Beginning SharePoint Communication Sites

Creating and Managing Professional Collaborative Experiences

Charles David Waghmare

Apress®

Beginning SharePoint Communication Sites: Creating and Managing Professional Collaborative Experiences

Charles David Waghmare
Mumbai, Maharashtra, India

ISBN-13 (pbk): 978-1-4842-4202-5   ISBN-13 (electronic): 978-1-4842-4203-2
https://doi.org/10.1007/978-1-4842-4203-2

Library of Congress Control Number: 2018965572

Managing Director, Apress Media LLC: Welmoed Spahr
Acquisitions Editor: Smriti Srivastava
Development Editor: Matthew Moodie
Coordinating Editor: Shrikant Vishwakarma

Cover designed by eStudioCalamar

Cover image designed by Freepik (www.freepik.com)

Distributed to the book trade worldwide by Springer Science+Business Media New York, 233 Spring Street, 6th Floor, New York, NY 10013. Phone 1-800-SPRINGER, fax (201) 348-4505, e-mail orders-ny@springer-sbm.com, or visit www.springeronline.com. Apress Media, LLC is a California LLC and the sole member (owner) is Springer Science + Business Media Finance Inc (SSBM Finance Inc). SSBM Finance Inc is a **Delaware** corporation.

For information on translations, please e-mail rights@apress.com, or visit http://www.apress.com/rights-permissions.

Apress titles may be purchased in bulk for academic, corporate, or promotional use. eBook versions and licenses are also available for most titles. For more information, reference our Print and eBook Bulk Sales web page at http://www.apress.com/bulk-sales.

Any source code or other supplementary material referenced by the author in this book is available to readers on GitHub via the book's product page, located at www.apress.com/978-1-4842-4202-5. For more detailed information, please visit http://www.apress.com/source-code.

Printed on acid-free paper

Dedication

"For the Lord gives wisdom; from His mouth come knowledge and understanding." – Proverbs 2:6

I would like to offer glory, praise, and honor to my God, Lord Jesus Christ, who gave me one more opportunity to write a book. I thank my God for being graceful to each one of us. God is Great!

My Dedication:

*My dearest parents—my father **Mr. David Genu Waghmare** and my mother **Mrs. Kamala David Waghmare**—who poured their blood and sweat to fulfill our needs and to keep us happy. Both are quite old in age now but are living with young spirits. God Bless them.*

*My sisters—**Mrs. Carol Kamble** and **Mrs. Mary Unhavane**—who always have been with me in good and bad times of my life. I am grateful for their love, support, and care.*

*My loveable nephews, **Kris**—A world of technology—and **Savio**—a passionate classical singer—in whom I see my childhood and my school days. I have always enjoyed having fun with them.*

*To—**Late Mr. Prashant Kamble** my brother-in-law who is not with us at this moment. We miss him every moment.*

Table of Contents

About the Author

Charles David Waghmare worked as a Global Yammer Community Manager from 2011 until mid-2018 with Capgemini. Previously he was a community manager of SAP-based communities at ATOS, where he managed communities using TechnoWeb 2.0—a Yammer-like platform. In this Communities of Practice (CoP) initiative, Charles was also responsible for managing community sites built in SharePoint On-premise. Further, at ATOS, Charles was the global rollout manager for a structured document-management system built in SharePoint On-premise.

The Capgemini Yammer network, one of the largest Yammer networks, was moderated by Charles to make Yammer a wonderful experience for each Capgemini user. At Capgemini, his responsibility was to manage the Yammer network containing over 135K+ users and an enterprise social knowledge management platform, built in Drupal called KM3.0, which also contained over 100K users. Charles contributed to build the next-generation knowledge-management platform called KM4.0 using SharePoint Online. Finally, Charles was part of Digital Workplace group at Capgemini, which dream to build Digital Workplace using Office 365 services such as Yammer, SharePoint Online and others.

About the Technical Reviewers

 **Cedric Oster** is a Microsoft Certified SharePoint Professional with 17 years' experience in IT with 12 years dedicated to Microsoft SharePoint Technologies. During an nine-year career in Capgemini London—two years as an independent SharePoint consultant/architect (London) and seven years at Capgemini Toulouse—he delivered some excellent solutions to a large variety of clients. He is responsible for Capgemini's offering on the Digital Workplace based on Office 365 and for the relationship with partners.

He works on a SharePoint project from start to finish and has successfully handled large projects as Technical Architect (TDA), offshore development lead, and information management consultant. He can also design logical and physical architecture, gather business requirements, install and configure SharePoint environments, administer SharePoint farms, and give well received end-user training and demos.

Cedric is able help clients write and implement SharePoint governance plans, information architecture, and taxonomy. Apart from this, he is responsible for a variety of successful SharePoint and Office 365 deliveries: two digital workplaces, five Intranet sites, two extranet sites, two My Sites (Enterprise Social Network), seven composite applications, one app (add-in), and one Internet site.

Kapil Bansal is a technical consultant at HCL Technologies, India. He has more than 10 years of experience in the IT industry. He has worked on Microsoft Azure Cloud Computing (PaaS, IaaS, and SaaS), Azure Stack, DevOps, Office 365, SharePoint, Release Management, ALM, ITIL, and Six Sigma. He has worked with companies like IBM India Pvt Ltd, NIIT Technologies, Encore Capital Group, and Xavient Software Solutions Noida and has served multiple clients based in the United States, the UK, and Africa like T-Mobile, WBMI, Encore Capital, and Bharti Airtel (India and Africa).

Acknowledgments

Manish Saxena, **Head KM and Collaboration at ATOS**, who gave me my first chance to work on SharePoint and offered me challenging projects to augment my career in SharePoint technology.

Mr. Madan Chakranarayan, for his love and care.

Miss Nisha Talwar, Engagement Manager at Capgemini, for her support during my difficult days.

Dear friends, Hanil Manghani, Vinay Pillai, and Swapnil Katare.

The Salvation Army, Matunga Corps, My Church. A special thanks to all members of my church, for their love and affection.

CHAPTER 1

SharePoint and Communication Sites: An Introduction

To begin, we take a glimpse of SharePoint Online and its associated functionalities—the Hub site, Team site, and Communication site. Once you have a good understanding, we move to SharePoint's community sites and explore various features in depth.

Introducing SharePoint Online

SharePoint Online is a service available under the Microsoft Office 365 product family. SharePoint Online is technically different from SharePoint. SharePoint Online is a cloud-based service that's part of the Office 365 product family and SharePoint is an on-premise version of SharePoint that can be installed in your environment in your own infrastructure, unlike SharePoint Online. With SharePoint Online, you can collaborate on work-related stuff and share content globally with your colleagues, partners, and customers. Internal sites, files uploaded, and any information hosted over SharePoint Online can be accessed easily from anywhere in the world, using mobile devices.

© Charles David Waghmare 2019
C. D. Waghmare, *Beginning SharePoint Communication Sites*,
https://doi.org/10.1007/978-1-4842-4203-2_1

Advantages and Disadvantages of SharePoint Online

Similar to SaaS, Software-as-as-Service products, SharePoint Online offers rich user experiences without an installation process. With a single click, users can explore rich content management and collaborative features that help them effectively perform their business tasks. Here are a few advantages of SharePoint Online.

- **Easy sharing and collaboration**—Empower sharing of content and collaboration between global teams. Offer space for people to share and collaborate information to remain updated. Enrich your Intranet and make it a place for sharing information.

- **Connect people**—Inform and communicate to your global employees. Publish breaking news and announcements with SharePoint dynamic pages.

- **Make decisions faster with intelligence**—The powerful search engine will help you find sites, attachments, and profiles. Built-in intelligence delivers relevant results to make decisions and discover vital information.

Besides these advantages, there are a few disadvantages of SharePoint Online as well:

- Due to the cloud factor in SharePoint Online, some companies have refrained from using it or they have decided to use a combination of on-premise and cloud versions

- There is less opportunity for customized development, as most of its features are available out of the box.

- There is no backend control and no content migration from other sources.

- Additional bandwidth is needed to access the platform.

- Integration with non-Microsoft products is not possible.

SharePoint Online Features

Up to this point, we talked about SharePoint Online and its power to facilitate content management and collaboration. In this section, we look at the features that make this possible and that create rich user experiences. These features are very easy to use.

File Storage: Provides options to upload, store, and share files.

External Sharing: Share files with your suppliers, partners, and clients who are outside your organization.

Content Management: Manage and organize content such as Web Content Management (WCM)—Intranet, news, articles, and posts—with metadata, records management, and a retention policy.

Team Sites: A dedicated place for your team to collaborate and share documents, news, and information to stay updated.

Communication Sites: Broadly communicate your message across your organization by publishing beautiful content to keep users informed and engaged in topics, events, and projects.

Intranets: Share your customer stories, leadership reviews, new customer wins, organization charts, and what is happening in your organization.

Mobile Apps: Access your content anywhere and anytime using mobile apps.

Automate Work: You can automate processes with alerts and workflows.

Discovery: Discover valuable content and people when you need to.

Search: Search and you will find what you want.

E-Discovery: Discover content in electronic format for legal and audit purposes.

Data Loss Prevention Capabilities (DLP): Use of advance DLP capabilities to monitor data loss and information security protection.

In-Place Hold: Prevent content from being edited or deleted.

Note   These images are the standard images used to denote these SharePoint features.

Using OneDrive (Me) and SharePoint (We)

Under the Office 365 product family, we have the OneDrive and SharePoint Online services, which have a similar purpose—to store files and documents uploaded by end users. So, two simple questions might arise in your mind—why are there two different services that perform the same job and should I save my file in OneDrive or in SharePoint? Although OneDrive and SharePoint Online both store files, they are totally different services and have different objectives

OneDrive is a place to store your private documents that only you intend to see, although you can share them if you want. For example, your salary slip document, company offer document, or employee feedback form. OneDrive is very similar to the "My Documents" folder or the hard drive on your desktop or laptop, where you keep all your own documents and files.

SharePoint on the other hand is different. We use SharePoint to collaborate and share content among different teams. Once a file is uploaded onto a SharePoint site, it becomes available to end users to view and edit if they have the rights. For example, all project-specific documents are not personal documents and therefore they are uploaded to the SharePoint site for end users to view and edit.

In short, OneDrive is used to store your own documents. However, it is possible to share documents from OneDrive with other users. It's *ME*. SharePoint is used to store files and documents that are intended to be collaborative. Documents uploaded onto SharePoint are for a group of users and not for a single person, so it is *WE*.

Exploring SharePoint Hub Sites

Before going into the details of SharePoint Communication sites, let's look at the different types of sites we can create on SharePoint Online. These sites differ in objectives from each other. There are three types of internal sites that can be created—you create a *Hub site* to connect, a *Team site* to collaborate, and a *Communication site* to broadcast information (see Figure 1-1). The Team and Communication sites can also be Hub sites. Besides these, you can create a traditional site collection system to manage your content.

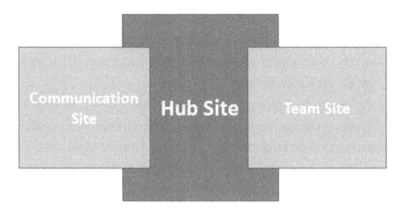

Figure 1-1. *Different SharePoint Online sites*

I already explained that a Communication site could be a Hub site, but the reverse is not always true. A Hub site might be a Communication site or a Team site, but not always. In this section, we explore Hub sites and learn about the benefits we get by creating a Hub site, which will be help us understand the concept of Communication sites with clarity.

Hub sites help you bring together different elements of the organizational Intranet into one single place. Hub sites are like the building blocks for your Intranet. Hub sites are also called the "connective tissue" that connects a collection of Team and Communications sites. The key principle of digital Intranets and social Intranets based on SharePoint is that each part of the Intranet should be created as a different site collection. This could be a Communication site or Team site with its own permissions, in order to manage it with diligence and accurate information, so that the latest information is available to the user community. A Hub site (most commonly created from a Communication site on SharePoint Online) should also be considered a different element of the Intranet that brings numerous other sites together.

In the past, multiple organizations used subsites as the connective tissue to bring different elements of their Intranet into one single place. Subsites were used to connect sites using the site collection's shared navigation. Such designs were not very flexible. SharePoint features such as retention and classification are required to be applied to all sites. This means that you must frequently enable such features for all site collections, even if they are applicable only to a unique site.

Change is likely to happen in your business whether you want it or not. Successful organizations know how to deal with change and even increase their business value through change. As change prevails and affects businesses, the content on the Intranet changes. As part of being in today's digital world, you are required to show the latest information quickly and in real-time. SharePoint's Hub sites play a vital role here, as they model relationships as links, rather than with a hierarchy or ownership model, so that you can adapt to changes in a dynamic, changing world.

Differences Among the Hub, Communication, and Team Sites

Table 1-1 explains the differences among the Hub, Communication, and Team sites.

Table 1-1. Comparing Hub, Communication, and Team Sites

	Team Site	Communication Site	Hub Site
Purpose	**Collaborate**	**Communicate**	**Connect**
Scenario	When you want to create a workplace where the entire team is based at an onshore/offshore location and is required to contribute to complete project deliverables, tract status of items tasks, share information with each other, and exchange new ideas. Team sites are connected to an Office 365 group where you utilize collaborative tools such as Microsoft teams to make collaboration possible.	When you want to communicate new customer wins, success stories, end year reviews, and new project pipelines, announce leadership teams, and publish CEO messages. You want to communicate news and information that cannot edited by end users. Such information can be shared on Yammer to build collaboration within the end user community	Creates a combined experience for end users by connecting collections of Communication sites and Team sites. Hub sites organize these family of sites to maintain a common look and feel.
Content Authors	All members are content authors who jointly create and edit content.	Dedicated group of content authors and large group of readers or content consumers.	Authors of the Team or Communication site who have configured these sites as Hub sites.

(continued)

Table 1-1. (*continued*)

	Team Site	Communication Site	Hub Site
Purpose	**Collaborate**	**Communicate**	**Connect**
Governance	Defined by the team involved in the collaboration.	Defined at the organizational level to ensure the correct communicate goes in the relevant messages.	Defined by the owner of the Team or Communication site who has configured them as Hub sites.
Created By	Site Owner	Site Owner	Global admin or SharePoint Admin in Office 365
Examples	1. Team site created to collaborate on day-to-day business challenges, propose solutions, and improve customer satisfaction. 2. To create user engagement during campaigns 3. To respond to customer RFPs.	1. Communication site created to communicate annual leadership reviews. 2. Communicate annual company results and company performance. 3. Share information about company events.	Hub site could exist for various departments, such as HR, IT, and various business units.

Examples of Hub Sites

Recall that the objective of a Team site is collaboration, the objective of a Communication site is to broadcast information or news, and the objective of a Hub site is to connect other sites to create a unified end user experience. As mentioned, a Hub site can be a communication or Team site. Further, Hub sites give you a combined experience of Team sites and Communication sites in terms of shared navigation and brand, content, search, and home destination for the hub. Let's take a closer look at some examples of Hub sites.

IT Department

Normally, an IT department has various divisions that work together to create an awesome user experience. IT departments have different internal divisions, such as application management, application monitoring, custom software development, server maintenance teams, database management teams, cloud services, hardware services, software installation team, and communication and quality team. These different teams work collaboratively in order to keep applications up and running.

From a user standpoint, it is very difficult to understand such complexity. Let's consider a scenario where an application is down and users are trying to connect to the relevant IT team to restore the application, but the users aren't sure how to do this. A Hub site for the IT department would provide user access to the most updated information of the branches in IT and thereby supply a proper way to contact the relevant department about an application issue (see Figure 1-2).

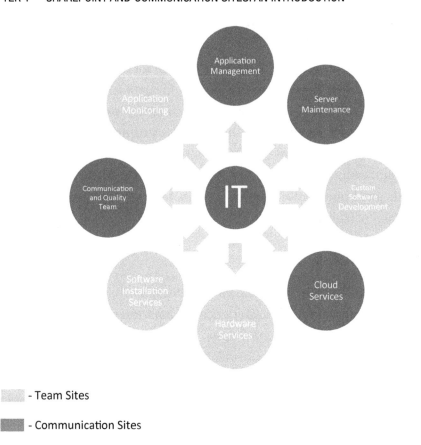

- Team Sites

- Communication Sites

Figure 1-2. *Hub site of an IT department*

Figure 1-2 shows a Hub site of a typical IT department. IT is a Communication site that connects Team sites—such as Software Installation Services and Hardware Services—that collaborate with end users to Communication sites—such as the Communication and Quality team—to provide a seamless experience when it comes to accessing information from the IT department.

Human Resources (HR) Department

A human resources department contains various departments. These
might include talent acquisition, sourcing and recruitment, payroll and
compensation, human resources (HR) partners, performance management,
and professional development. Any new employee is likely to get lost when
trying to find onboarding resources if there is no Hub site in place. Normally,
a buddy is assigned to the new employee to provide access to onboarding
resources. If you have a human resources Hub site updated with the latest
information, there is no need to assign a buddy—at least for this reason!

Figure 1-3 shows an HR Hub site that's a Team site. It connects other
Team sites—such as sourcing and recruitment, talent acquisition, and HR
partners—to Communication sites such as payroll and compensation,
professional development, and performance management.

- Team Sites

- Communication Sites

Figure 1-3. *Hub site of HR department*

Exploring Communication Sites

After understanding the differences between Communication sites and Hub sites, it's time to explore SharePoint Communication sites independently. A SharePoint Online Communication site is a place to share information, such as news, reports, statuses, and events, in a visually captivating format with a large audience that's part of your organization.

SharePoint Communication sites are ideal for internal collaboration during internal campaigns, news and insights, business highlights, year-end leaders review, and new customer wins. To jumpstart user collaboration, Communication sites provide configurable templates. These templates make your life easier while communicating messages to large audiences in a short amount of time.

Communication sites are accessible across various devices. Users can consume information using mobile device available through SharePoint apps. It's easy to access, engage with, and create content for Communication sites from any device. SharePoint Communication sites are awesome ways to share information and collaborate in your organization. Creating SharePoint sites has become a very simple process, with available out-of-box features and zero coding effort. Communication sites are predestined to transform your current communication channels and improve your end users' experiences.

You can create a beautiful Communication site in seconds using the SharePoint home available in Office 365. Then you can improve your methods of communicating and collaborating with large audiences, integrate your existing collaboration channels into a SharePoint Communication site, and plenty more. Communication sites allow people to create and share periodic updates beyond email.

Steps to Create SharePoint Communication Sites

Here are the steps to create SharePoint Communication sites. These steps are simple and easy to understand.

1. Sign in to Office 365.

2. From the app launcher available on the top left of any Office 365 service (or access www.portal. office.com), select the SharePoint tile. At the top of the SharePoint home page, you will see the Create Site button and then the Create Communication Site option, as shown in Figures 1-4 and 1-5.

Figure 1-4. *Option to create a site, whereby you can create a Team or Communication site*

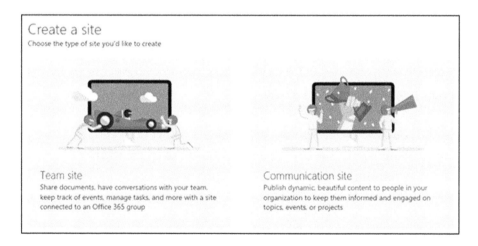

Figure 1-5. *Choose a Team or Communication site*

3. Select one of the following site designs (see Figure 1-6):

    • Topic to share information such as news, events,
       and other content.

    • Showcase to use photos or images to showcase a
       product, team, or event.

    • Blank to create your own design.

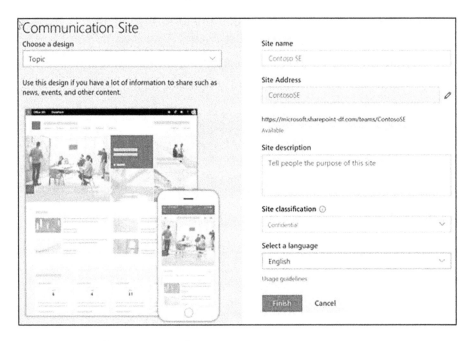

Figure 1-6. *Choose a site design*

4. Finally, update the site name, site classification, and
    language as needed. Then click Finish to create your
    Communication site.

What Do Communication Sites Include?

You can create a blank Communication site from SharePoint Online and use the following design options, which come with set of default webparts to design your Communication site. You can add, remove, or re-order webparts whenever you want. Here are three design options:

- Topic: To publish information such as news, events, and announcements

- Showcase: To display photos or images taken during events, conferences, or customer visits

- Blank: To create your own design

At the top of the Communication sites, there is a link to add a list, a Document Library, a page, a new post, and web app to the site, as shown in Figure 1-7.

Figure 1-7. *Add a new list, Document Library, page, news post, or web app to your Communication site*

To design your Communication site, let's look in detail at the different options available to design sites. When you select an option (Topic, Showcase, or Blank), you see several webparts available for you to design your site.

- **Topic**—Under Topic, you have the Hero, News, Events, and Highlighted Content webparts.

    - **Hero**—Generate focus and visual interest on your page. A maximum of five items can be added to a Hero webpart. You can also add images. The Hero webpart is included by default in all Communication sites. Once you click the Hero webpart, it appears prepopulated with images, text, and links and you can modify them or add your own. This webpart has a tiled layout with five tiles and you can modify them from one to five (see Figure 1-8).

Figure 1-8. *An example Hero webpart*

- **News**—Keep your team in the loop and continue to engage with them with successful stories using the News webpart. Using this webpart, you can create eye-catching posts like new customer wins, company-wide announcements, and project status updates with enriched graphical information. See Figure 1-9.

Figure 1-9. *A News webpart*

- **Events**—Display upcoming events using the Events webpart, as shown in Figure 1-10.

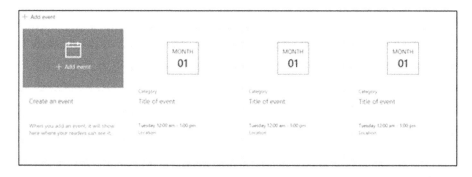

Figure 1-10. *An Events webpart*

- **Highlighted Content**—This webpart displays content from the Document Library or from certain sites to highlight relevance of content. You can use this feature to highlight your company employee policy document or code of conduct, for example.

- **Showcase**— The Showcase design option is available in communicate sites, and it has its own set of default webparts.

  - **Image Gallery**—To share a variety of images.

- **Blank**—When you start with a blank Communication site, there is no need to remove webparts that you do not need. You just choose your page layout and add the webparts you want.

Note   The images shown here are demo images and do not link to any production SharePoint site. They are simply used to describe the Communication site features.

Summary

In this chapter, we gained a good understanding of the Hub, Communication, and Team sites. Further, we also saw the steps to create Communication sites and various design options available with a set of default webparts. With this understanding, we move to the next chapter, which focuses only on the collaboration and communication aspect using Communication sites.

CHAPTER 2

Effectively Communicate and Collaborate Using Communication Sites

In the first chapter, we saw an overview of how you can use Communication sites and Hub sites in SharePoint Online and some situations in which you need a Hub or Communication site. Then, we looked at some SharePoint Online features. In this chapter, we describe various use cases where communicating through SharePoint Communication sites is better. We also see how Communication sites are useful to communicate to small and large groups and create scope for collaboration.

Also, we see how we can send effective communication to big groups and communications related to campaigns, announcements, and leadership teams, thereby creating new communication and collaborative channels. First, we look at the vital difference between communication and collaboration.

© Charles David Waghmare 2019
C. D. Waghmare, *Beginning SharePoint Communication Sites*,
https://doi.org/10.1007/978-1-4842-4203-2_2

Communication and Collaboration

Workforces around the world use various systems to communicate and collaborate in order to achieve their business objectives. Multiple technologies are launched to make communication and collaboration easy and efficient. In this section, we explore the basics of communication and collaboration and check out why they need to coexist in any organization.

- **Communication**—We understand that, in this process, two or more people are involved. Communication involves people expressing their feelings, ideas, needs, and questions that are comprehensible to others. It is clearly understandable to the other person or group of people in such a way that they are able to respond to it. It's very important that the language used in the communication process be understandable to both parties. Communication can be face-to-face, over mobile devices, over Skype calls, and via texts/emails. Communication is an important aspect of being a good professional. If you have strong communication skills, you speak, read, write, and understand what is necessary to do your job.

Figure 2-1. *Telephone used for communication. Royalty free image available at* https://www.freeimages.com/photo/old-phone-1313726

- **Collaboration**—This is action-oriented communication where two or more people work together to solve problems. Communication is essential in collaboration, as when communication is clear, people understand the message and work accordingly. Collaboration requires a common goal or objective. If a team works collaboratively, this means they communicate very well and work as per expectations. They can then achieve good results in collaboration. Collaboration always focuses on the team or on a group of individuals to achieve goals.

Figure 2-2. *A team works collaboratively to achieve desired results. Copyright free image available at* https://www.pexels.com/search/team/

The difference between communication and collaboration is subtle and they are intertwined. For successful collaboration, you need to have communication and for communication to take place, there is an element of collaboration. Communication initially begins from one side and then the other party decides whether they can respond. But in collaboration, all parties must communicate. Traditional Intranets that communicate information to employees do not have the opportunity to react or respond. In such a situation, communication is one sided. With a traditional Intranet example, we can infer that communication can be one sided, as traditional Intranets existed to communicate information in one way. There was no other way to capture reactions based on information that was communicated. Communication sometimes is casual and doesn't require action. A casual discussion over dinner or coffee might not have a goal or purpose, yet we have casual discussion to express our minds and feel better. However, collaboration always has a purpose.

In this chapter, we discover effective ways to communicate and collaborate using SharePoint Communication sites. Communication in an organization is crucial because it helps employees know what happened and what will happen in the organization. If we do not communicate to employees there will be chaos in the organization and, as a result, employees will not remain in sync with each other. When employees are able to collaborate, business objectives are achieved. Today many organizations invest huge amounts of money to continuously improve employee communication and collaboration. Not only this, but employers are building digital experiences for communication and collaboration because both of these are necessary for business success. Here are some reasons why communication and collaboration should both exist in your organization and should get better every day.

- Regular employee communication is essential to know what's happening in the organization.

- Collaboration platforms such as SharePoint Communication sites and Yammer help employees collaborate, connect, and share business-related problems.

- Two-way communication is necessary to create employee engagement and understand their feedback on published communication.

- Collaboration is essential on any news, update, or announcement to understand employee reactions.

- Open and transparent communication creates clarity of business objectives in an organization.

- Collaboration drives the action plan to drive the business objectives.

- Leadership communication is vital to employees, as they often prefer to know the leadership's views.

- Collaboration creates a connection between leaders and employees.

- Through communication, employees gain a common understanding of the organizational initiatives.

- Collaboration helps to drive these initiatives.

- Communication creates a common culture.

- Collaboration helps sustain the common culture.

- In global setups, employee communication exists in several languages.

- Collaboration helps bridge cross-culture boundaries.

Now, let's look at some use cases where effective collaboration and communication through SharePoint become simple.

Communication and Collaboration Use Cases

We will take different departments into consideration, identify their pain areas, and list the solutions with the help of a Communication site. Every organization has departments that are based on the same office. Global companies have their departments spread across countries and continents. Considering the background of the global organization and the different languages, cultures, and diversities, it becomes very challenging to communicate in one common and understandable language. Internal communication teams work hard to make sure that all communication goes through precise and unique filters for maximum understanding. It is also challenging to have people from different backgrounds collaborate to achieve business objectives.

Human Resources

Let's start with the human resources department. The human resources department has various subdepartments in it, such as Sourcing, Recruitment, Business Partners, Compensation, Employee Onboarding, Benefits, Leave Management, and Exit Formalities. Different subdepartments result in plenty of information needing to be synchronized, so that their Human Resources dashboards remain up-to-date. With such diversity and a global presence, human resources deals with many different problems on a day-to-day basis, as follows:

- **Must be compliant with local employment laws and regulation**—All global organizations are going through this problem, as work permit rules, labor laws, regulations are changing and differ among countries. It is very important that the immigration and human resources departments are in sync before they can hire or deploy employees

- **Dealing with change**—With growing businesses, their strategies, culture, and internal processes change. Some employees have a hard time adopting to these changes. During the acquisition process, multiple changes take place. As a result, some people are able to adapt and others aren't. As a consequence, there is loss of productivity.

- **Lack of leadership development**—One international study showed that more than one third of companies are performing an average job implementing leadership development programs. A full 30 percent of companies admitted they were below average when it comes to performing leadership development jobs.

- **Poor training programs**—There has always been a mismatch in training offerings for employees who are in the office versus those who deal directly with customers. Employees tend to invest more in training employees in the office. Employees who are on the front lines are some of best employees. If you investment more in them, they will stay longer and be a big asset to your company.

- **Diversity in the workplace**—Generations, ethnics, and different cultures all create challenges for human resources.

These are just a few challenges that the human resources department comes across. Do these Communication sites help overcome these human resources challenges? The answer is yes.

Build an Internal Website for the Sub-departments

SharePoint Communication sites allow each subdepartment to build an internal website for its employees. Today, most organizations have an Intranet and each department has a dedicated area where they dump information, which cannot be found easily by users. Subdepartments have no dedicated space and, as a result, people from such teams are not easily traceable. With Communication sites, subdepartments can manage their information on their own. They can publish news, announcements, policies, training programs, immigration rules, and others. Subdepartments can host documents in the Document Library and share them with end users. Not only this, but videos, PowerPoint presentations, and charts can be added to each page. If each subdepartment can work hand-in-hand with its end users, subdepartments will be visible and they will have a greater role to play in the organization. All subdepartmental sites can be connected to the human resources Hub site so that you have a centralized structure of sites under one main Hub site.

The human resources department and its subdepartments can be visible and accessible using Communication sites and, as a result, subdepartments can continue to grow hand-in-hand with end users. No more contacting these subdepartments through a distribution list or raising a ticket in the help desk. You instead visit the subdepartment site and find the available information and contact section, which is a default webpart.

Internal Communications

This department is a core department of corporate communications. The internal communication team (IC) publishes news, announcements, and updates from various departments and locations. IC is made up of a communication manager and an editorial team that creates communication for the entire organization. The IC team is split into countries and global teams. The IC team uses the corporate Intranet as their platform for communicating with the organization. The better the Intranet platform, the more structured communication can be published and the better the feedback. Despite being a global team and being the center of focus, this department goes through various problems, such as those:

- **Existence of communication flow from top to bottom only**—The content of this team comes from the person who has a strategic role in the organization. This person could be the strategic business unit head, a departmental head, the chief technology officer, a country head, or the CEO of the organization. The IC team approaches such people from a strategic role and creates news around this, which is published on the Intranet. However, communication should go from bottom to top and also in the horizontal direction, so that management can understand the expectations of the people who report to them.

- **Lack of employee focus**—Some organizations do not allow all employees to voice their feedback, provide suggestions, and propose improvements. Normally such ideas come from specialized teams or third-party agencies. If all employees are given an opportunity to be part of the communication journey, organizational transformation will not remain a challenge as it is today.

- **Last minute communication**—There are various situations, due to heavy rains or snowfall, in which roads are blocked, or due to a local strike, people cannot commute to the office. In those cases, if there is urgent information to be shared, such as leadership changes, company stock changes, or a natural disaster, this is often communicated through emails. Today's Intranet does not allow you to publish last-minute communications.

- **IC for digital users**—Today's spending on Intranet resources has diminished because organizations are more interested in their return on investment. Intranet benefits are intangible and cannot be measured through profit and loss, as projects can. There are systems such as emails, Intranet, VOIP, exchange servers, and others, for which we never bothered to have a return on investment. We need them to run the business effectively, which can be proven by closing them down for one day.

- **Making IC competitive**—Today we have different
  forms of communication in organizations, such as
  Yammer, Teams, Skype, and Outlook. People-to-people
  communication is faster than IC. For example, if a new
  CEO is appointed, this news is rapidly spread through
  non-IC channels and the IC information is published
  after it is well known. There is a need now for IC to
  revamp its strategy, improve the technology, and build
  better processes to communicate effectively.

These challenges can be easily resolved using Communication sites.
In the first challenge, existence of communication only in the top to
bottom fashion, for example, you can use Communication sites to make
communication two-way and therefore more collaborative. Using the
Yammer webpart embedded into your sites, such two-way communication
can be facilitated. The moment news is published, users can voice their
opinions through the Yammer group embedded into the site. With
Communication sites, you can meet the second challenge of IC not being
focused on employees. This collaborative experience can also be added
using a Yammer group or a Team site. You can use the Embed webpart to
add content from other sources such as social media sites and business
content sites such as the content loop and make them available on the
Communication site page. You can use the Kindle webpart to share
previews of books and use Microsoft forms to create survey quizzes and
polls. Out-of-the-box webparts available in the Communication sites will
help you create user engagement and involve users in the communication
journey.

The third challenge is of last-minute communications by IC during
natural calamities or local problems. This can also be easily managed by
Communication sites. SharePoint Administrator or Office 365 can easily
create a communicate site and, within 10 minutes, your Communication
site will be ready with important news that you want to share. There are

famous SharePoint Communication sites published by Microsoft that demonstrate creation of up-to-date communication in just 10 minutes. This is possible due to the number of webparts it has and no specialized communication is needed unless there is a specific requirement.

Today, most Intranet users are also social media users and part of the latest technology trend such as Cloud, Azure, and others. Therefore, it is important that we give our user community a similar experience inside the organization. SharePoint Communication sites are available within the Office 365 product family. Once you get this service, your organization does not have to manage it; Microsoft will manage the service and your organization will be the consumer. No more headaches monitoring, database upgrades, patch fixing, maintenance windows, server upgrades, and 24/7 support. This is all done by Microsoft. You focus on using this service effectively. Not only this, but SharePoint Online provides a mobile app that users can use to view organizational communication at any time.

The internal communication strategy needs to be revamped, as users have access to modern internal tools that help them spread messages faster than the IC team does. With Communication sites, various ideas can be implemented using design options such as the Hero, News, Events, and Blank webparts. With access to the Microsoft image library, you can use nice images and make users feel good. Besides, using the Embed webpart, you can show feeds from external sites, use the Yammer webpart for collaboration, link webparts to external links, use power apps for customized internal apps, and much more. It is time to make your Intranets digital, social, and competitive by revamping your old internal strategy, which focused only on content. The time has come to offer digital, collaborative, mobile platforms to your employees.

IT Department

Let's now talk about one of the most important departments in the organization, which is crucial for business, but whenever it comes to their own communication or transformation, it is often ignored. This is the Information Technology (IT) department, which provides and supports the software and hardware, so that the business can deliver on customer expectations. But when it comes to contacting people from the IT department, whether it is L1 or L3 support, we have been forced to raise a ticket. Many do not bother to raise a ticket and instead walk into the support team's cubical. There is a genuine problem of communication and collaboration between the IT department and the user community. Let's discuss some of these problems:

- **Inaccessibility of IT documents**—IT departments support the internal application, including changes and enhancements, which is technology dependent. So, we have a huge team here already. Parts of the team look after the datacenter, handle information security, procure the IT hardware and software, and manage IT governance and licences. Their standard documents are usually inaccessible. For example, if you want security guidelines for a Software as a Service product, you often need to go to multiple people before you can find them.

- **Invisible services**—The IT department provides numerous services such as L1 support (basic hardware and software support) and coordinate vendor support. The IT team also has an L2 and L3 support team that manages escalations and more complex issues. Could the service management team provide services such as database, application hosting, and application upgrades? There is also a delivery team

33

that provides similar services to external customers. Nobody is aware that we have redundant teams that are actually providing similar services, as there is no place in the organization where the IT team and their subdepartments can display services they can offer. In IT, standardizations such as ITIL, IS20K, and others are strictly followed but after achieving compliance in an audit, they do not have a platform to showcase their expertise or experience gained.

- **Lack of communication**—The IT help desk communicates either through a ticketing tool or they use Skype to communicate with end users. Whenever the IT team sends communications, they are linked to application outages, downtime information, software upgrades and others, but these are general communications. No user-specific communication is written down on Yammer, Teams, or the SharePoint site.

- **Lack of collaboration**—Collaboration between the IT department and the user community can be better and stronger. People rely on ticketing tools too much. Some organizations have started using Yammer as a social help desk to collaborate with end users about their issues. That way, the delivery teams interact to deliver business expectations the same way the IT teams and user community should collaborate.

- **Lack of employee empowerment**—Teams from the IT department are never given a chance to run a campaign, announce achievements, and perform fun related activities. We cannot figure out the precise reason for this trend in most of these organizations, but responsibility does lie with the leadership teams.

The IT department has plenty of challenges to be visible and collaborative and to have strong communication. But with SharePoint Communication sites things have become simple for them. The IT department and its subdepartments can now create their internal sites on which they showcase their services, applications they support, and point of contacts. With the help of the Document Library, all the subdepartments can upload and share documents with the user community. Further, they can insert attachments such as Word docs, Excel sheets, and PDFs in their site pages. This resolves the first and second challenges mentioned earlier.

To collaborate and communicate with end users, IT subdepartments can use site pages. Various webparts can used to build visually appealing communication and Yammer will facilitate collaboration. SharePoint Communication sites will give employees an opportunity for a digital and mobile experience. Everything you need to develop a digital and collaborative experience is available through webparts. For employee empowerment, with leadership support, the IT department can execute campaigns, run surveys and polls for their own subdepartments, and create their own Yammer groups for collaboration and outreach. In this way, the IT department can become stronger, more visible, and more accessible without additional cost.

Facilities Management

Let's look at a final way that Communication sites provide a better experience for collaborating and communicating. Let's take the example of the facilities management department. This includes support functions and facility such as admin assistants, receptionists, program manager officers (PMO), and facility managers. Such support functions are normally not considered on the Intranet pages. Let's look at some challenges that these support personnel face:

- **Invisible department**—They maintain a low profile in the organization and are not seen in communications. But ideally, all departments should be visible in the sense that there should be a portal that contains a list of services they provide and a point of contact for them.

- **No acknowledgement**—Facility teams do an excellent job to ensure workplaces are clean, tidy, and up to standard. They work hard, yet don't get much acclaim and are not typically part of the recognition program.

- **Lack of training and development**—For support function team members, there is no career development as we have for others. There is no training program, and there are no workshops conducted for them. In short, there is an absence of collaboration due to which they are unable to get promoted.

- **Limited access**—Support employees are often not given enough access to major internal applications. In my experience, employees from the support function were not given corporate mail addressed to reduce cost and they were operating with general email addresses and mail accounts. If the situation is limited, an employee focus strategy will never become possible.

SharePoint Communication sites are created for all types of employees, so that they can effectively collaborate and communicate. With SharePoint Communication sites, internal sites allow all participating departments to communicate and highlight their services. Employees, after reading their news, announcements, and updates, will acknowledge their work and share praise and appreciation. Integrating with Yammer will help with collaboration between support functions and their service consumers. Training and workshops can be made available on the support function portal. The organization has to take a stand and explore how Communication sites can provide opportunities for each employee in the organization to contribute to their department and organization.

Communication Sites for Smaller and Larger Groups

In this section, we see how SharePoint Communication sites are useful for effective collaboration and communication in smaller and larger groups. Let's start with smaller groups. Smaller groups could be a project or small like-minded community or a team with a specific task. Here are some communication problems that smaller teams face:

- Lack or absence of a virtual place to communicate

- No communication strategy planned for smaller groups

- Small team comfortable speaking over the phone and one-on-one rather than in teams

- Lack of guidance on communication improvement

- Small team in a global setting prefers face-to-face workshops rather continuous communication

- Email communication is often preferred

Smaller teams may be relatively small but the communication aspect is vital and this where SharePoint Communication sites make communication smooth in smaller teams. Smaller teams can create a site for their internal communication and objectives. This can be private and can embed a Yammer group for collaboration. Sites will create transparency and will reduce one-to-one communication. Agile Scrum Master can use Communication sites effectively. After the daily standup meeting, the status of artifacts can be published on the Communication site.

The team's task list can be shared through Communication sites. Useful presentations and documents can be attached to the sites using the File Viewer webpart. Minutes from a meeting can be shared by posting over the Communication sites. Events can be organized, team planning can be shared, and more stuff can done using Communication sites. They will enhance the way smaller teams work and communicate.

Bigger teams often have communication problems as well. Normally, a distribution list is created for communication, but this can be replaced by Communication sites and used in the most efficient and professional manner. Once a project is over, such sites can be deleted. Here are some challenges that bigger teams face when communicating:

- Lack of feedback channels, which leads to areas of improvement or growth being hidden.

- Preferred email communication.

- A combination of generation Y users and traditional users, which leads to a conflict of communication mediums.

- Less communication with new people joining the team.

- Sharing project collaterals if the size is too big.

- Culture barriers if the team is global.

Communication sites will make life easier for bigger teams. Distribution lists can simply be deleted and Communication sites can be used instead. All project reports, documents, planning notes, general content, and news should be stored on the Communication site. The project manager of a bigger team can share project planning, daily task schedules, and meeting updates on the site.

Execute Campaigns Using Communication Sites

Campaigns are events managed by the organization to improve user engagement and communicate business objectives. For any campaign, its reach is very important. Email was a primitive source for campaign communication and for sharing marketing collaterals. However, not all of the employees will read campaign related emails if they are getting multiple emails everyday and, as result, the reaction is minimized. Besides, due to the large size of market collaterals, email servers can hang. Therefore, you go through plenty of challenges when sharing content.

With Communication sites, campaign communication and collaboration has become straightforward and involves fewer challenges. Here are the steps to launch a campaign using Communication sites:

- Create a campaign-specific Communication site and keep it public if the campaign is global.

- Design your site page using the Hero, News, Highlighted Content, and Blank design options

- Using the Planner webpart, display campaign planning.

- Add the Yammer webpart to add Yammer groups linked to campaigns.

- Choose a visually captivating image from your site page.

- Add the Document Library to share files.

- Schedule campaign events using the Event webpart.

- Publish campaign communication.

- Make campaign announcements.

- Share marketing collaterals.

- Publish campaign reports using the power BI.

- Add links using the Link webpart.

- Share site links through email and the Yammer group.

- Once the campaign is closed, you can archive or delete the site.

SharePoint Communication Sites for Leadership Communication

In today's world, leadership has been transformed and leaders are expected to have excellent communication skills. Leaders usually publish their messages during the kick-off year, yearly reviews, new wins, and organizational road map. Some leaders with expertise in a certain area, for example the chief technology officer, will start a new technology series to communicate with their employees. If we create a Communication site for each leader, the leaders will be able to communicate with their employees on a regular basis and get feedback. SharePoint Communication sites can lessen the gap between leaders and employees.

Summary

In this chapter, we discovered the different departments and their challenges linked to communication and collaboration, which can be resolved using Communication sites. We also learned that this feature can be effectively used during campaigns and for leadership communication. In the next chapter, we see how Communication sites create collaborative experiences for the end users.

CHAPTER 3

Build Collaborative Experiences for End Users

In the previous chapter, we learned how SharePoint Communication sites make a difference in enriching the communication and collaborative experience. We saw some use cases where different departments went through different challenges, yet SharePoint Communication sites can address these issues. In this chapter, you learn how to build collaborative experiences for your end users with the help of SharePoint Communication sites.

SharePoint Communication sites were designed to communicate faster and in a more visually appealing way. To generate a collaborative experience, Yammer is used to integrate with Communication sites. With the Yammer webpart, it is easy to collaborate on information communicated using Communication sites. To begin with, we will introduce what Yammer is, what its benefits are, and how it helps you collaborate, and finally, we will discover how SharePoint Communication sites—along with Outlook and Yammer—create a collaborative experience for your end users.

© Charles David Waghmare 2019
C. D. Waghmare, *Beginning SharePoint Communication Sites*,
https://doi.org/10.1007/978-1-4842-4203-2_3

Introducing Yammer

Yammer is enterprise social networking platform used to collaborate, connect, and share business related activities. Yammer creates a social culture and facilitates social collaboration. If you want a point of contact, a reusable solution, want to share learnings and post events or conferences, share content with global teams, and connect with leadership teams, Yammer is the ideal platform. Many organizations have used Yammer as their social Intranet. You might ask why you would need Yammer when you already use email and Instant Messaging (IM), perhaps. Email and IM are great technologies, but they are the previous generation of communication tools.

Yammer is better than email because it's:

- **Discoverable**—Information that would otherwise be buried in people's email inboxes is in a central searchable feed. Furthermore, because Yammer threads are hosted, everyone is kept on the same page, and nobody is left out of the loop.

- **Faster**—Yammer is real-time, and messages are shorter and less formal than email.

- **More powerful**—Rapidly disseminate information to large groups and get answers to questions even when you don't know who to ask, all without spamming others. Yammer becomes more powerful as more people join, letting you tap into the collective mind of your organization.

- **Unaffected by spam**—Unlike email, you can't be spammed by external sources.

- **More controllable**—Messages can't be forwarded outside your Yammer network. Only employees can access them. When employees leave the company, they are immediately unable to access your company's Yammer network, but their previous contributions remain for the benefit of others.

Yammer is better than IM because it's:

- **Discoverable**—Conversations are centralized where everyone can see them, and others are encouraged to participate. With IM, on the other hand, only the people who were directly involved are aware that the conversation ever took place.

- **Persistent and searchable**—Yammer threads are automatically archived and searchable. By contrast, IM conversations are ephemeral and aren't searchable by others in your organization.

- **Always on**—You can receive Yammer messages even when you're offline, and they'll be instantly delivered to you the next time you check your feed (from any Internet-capable device).

- **More powerful**—You can hold real-time private conversations—just like you can with IM—but also have group and inter-company conversations that spread ideas and engage all members of your team.

- **Under Your control**—Company admins control membership, security settings, look-and-feel, the usage policy, and keywords as well as export all the data for eDiscovery and backup. While technologies like Yammer will eventually replace email and IM, we realize that this shift won't happen overnight. That's why Yammer integrates with these technologies—you can consume and create Yammer messages via email as well as through IM technologies like Google Talk or Jabber.

Why Use Yammer?

You'll be more productive and connected to your colleagues:

- Choose what information you consume and Yammer keeps it organized for you.

- People separated by organizational or geographical boundaries can now find and help each other.

- Easily monitor progress and stay up-to-date on what people are doing and talking about.

- Reduce overlap and duplicated effort—colleagues are more aware of each other's tasks.

- Make decisions faster with fewer phone calls and no more long email chains.

- Stay connected to what's happening at work with Yammer on your mobile device.

It's a great source of relevant information:

- Ask a question and get quick answers from experts within your company.

- Tap into your organization's collective mind by soliciting many ideas quickly and collaboratively solving difficult problems.

- Search a complete archive of messages, profiles, and tags.

- Discover valuable information in past discussions even if you weren't part of them.

- Retain the knowledge of former colleagues—their ideas and answers remain searchable.

- Discover influential people in your organization who can help you accomplish your goals.

- Get up to speed faster if you're new to your organization (up to a 10x improvement).

- Find and contact people easily.

- Discover how people are connected to you in your company's org-chart, which can make your company a better place to work.

Make your company feel smaller and allow good ideas to come from anywhere:

- Increase participation in discussions.

- Document and get credit for your ideas.

- Gain greater visibility into who you work with and their unique backgrounds.

- Start conversations and build relationships more easily.

- Promote a more collaborative culture in which information flows more freely and openly.

- Flatten the corporate hierarchy and break silos between departments and divisions.

It's better than email:

- Communicate in real-time, faster, shorter, and less formally than email.

- Rapidly disseminate information to a large number of people.

- Reduce miscommunication because conversations are more visible.

- Get answers to questions even when you don't know who to ask.

- Discover information that would otherwise be buried in other people's email inboxes.

- Start a group discussion without spamming people.

- Becomes more powerful the more you use it and the more people who join.

- Unlike email, you can't be spammed by external sources.

- Messages can't be forwarded outside your company's Yammer network.

Saves you time:

- Reduce your email burden—customers have reported as much a 60% reduction in email.

- Eliminate mailing lists and the maintenance associated with them.

- Easy setup, as there is nothing to install.

- Your customers and external partners can use it too.

- Create spin-off Yammer communities around a specific project, customer, topic etc.

- Communities are private and have their own messages, members, administrators, etc.

- Your company's internal Yammer network remains private and employee-only.

- Jump-start collaborations by introducing teams and getting discussions going much faster.

- Maintain a closer relationship with your customers and increase their satisfaction.

On Yammer, you can create different types of engagements. Here is the list of engagements that you can do and their corresponding benefits.

Engagement	Benefits
Team collaboration/share content	Will keep global teams up-to-date
Share business/technical issues	Get solutions faster; works like a network
Welcome/on-board new joiners	Speed up on-boarding and build connections
Publish internal opportunities	Hub for internal opportunities

(*continued*)

Engagement	Benefits
Build a social help desk	Answer end user queries and post info/news
Create leadership engagement	Will build connections with leaders
Ask for feedback and suggestions	Get ideas for improvement
Use Yammer over DL	Make communication social and collaborative
Plan a YamJam (brain storming session with teams) and a YamChat (Q&A session with leadership team)	Discover solutions by brainstorming and building connections with leadership teams through Q&A sessions
Make Yammer your communication channel	Share most relevant info/news
Share experience and stories	Build connections and visibility
Praise users	Create employee engagement
Run your internal campaigns	Brand tools, process, and teams

Yammer versus SharePoint

You may wonder whether to use Yammer or SharePoint for collaboration and document management. For project collaboration, should you create a group on Yammer or create a SharePoint Communication site? We will try to answer these questions in this section.

When Yammer was acquired by Microsoft in 2013, it was the only product of Microsoft that operated in the Software as a Service (SaaS) model. After a few years, with the birth of Office 365, we saw a transformation and services offered by Microsoft became SaaS, with the exception of SharePoint Server 2016. Microsoft publicly announced in *Redmond Magazine* that Yammer would be the future of enterprise social.

Office 365 includes two options for enterprise social features in SharePoint Online—Yammer and Newsfeed. The SharePoint Administrator chooses one of those options. You can turn it off or on Yammer in SharePoint using the SharePoint Online admin center. To perform this action, you need the Office 365 global admin of your tenant.

To build social collaboration, most companies use Yammer. If there are some concerns about cloud security or local labor laws from a cloud perspective, people use the on-premise version of SharePoint. SharePoint Online being hosted in the cloud sometime raises similar concerns with some customers.

Yammer by nature creates and encourages discussions, forms communities of like-minded using Yammer groups, shares content with global teams, and builds user engagements. However, it has some weakness such as it does not have a structured document management feature. SharePoint allows you to create workflows, but Yammer does not. SharePoint is available in on-premise and SaaS versions as well. Yammer exists in SaaS only. Let's draw some comparisons between Yammer and SharePoint.

	Yammer	SharePoint
Provioioning	Scrvicc undcr Office 3C5	Service under Office 365 as SharePoint Online and an on-premise version also available
Objective	Enterprise Social Collaboration	Enterprise Content Management
Features	Create and manage discussions	Create sites for managing documents and manage permission for sites
	Create groups for team collaboration	
	User profile	User profile
	Create hash topics, i.e., social tagging	Options to design community pages
		Document Library
	Activity streams, usage policy	Image library

(*continued*)

	Yammer	SharePoint
Administrator	Office 365 Global Admin	Office 365 Global Admin and SharePoint Online admin site administrator for on-premise SharePoint version
Search	Standalone searches	Enterprise search and can search documents from Yammer, OneDrive, and SharePoint
Examples	Launch campaigns using Yammer, facilitate project collaboration using Yammer	Create structured document management systems using SharePoint, create knowledge pools such as SlideShare using SharePoint
Customization	Not available	You can do more customization in the on-premise version of SharePoint
One-to-one message	Skype for business (Online Yammer Chat is being deprecated)	Skype for business

Imagine you are running a global project and different teams are working in different locations. These teams need to update different process documents so that the latest updates are captured in a document and teams around the world can use these updates. For such an activity, Yammer will not be useful, as it will help employees collaborate. Such a situation requires a document management system that allows users to manage documents using features such as version control, check-in/check-out features, and more:

- Features such as version control, auditing, records management, and workflows for effectively managing documents

- Creating web pages, adding rich media, and adding multiple pages for web content management

- Image and document libraries and calendars to manage events

Most of these features are available in the form of webparts, which are easy to use and deploy. For these features you can build Intranets, internal websites for departments and projects that manage documents. With Yammer webpart, you can use Yammer as a place for social collaboration in your SharePoint Communication, Team site, or any site you create in SharePoint. In other words, you make Yammer the default social network on SharePoint Online.

Activate Yammer from SharePoint Online

In Office 365, there are two options available for enterprise social features in SharePoint—Yammer and Newsfeed. A minimum plan of Office 365 includes Yammer, but if you still do not have it, contact Microsoft and get a Yammer network for your organization. The SharePoint Online administrator has an option to choose Newsfeed or Yammer for enterprise social collaboration in SharePoint Online (see Figure 3-1).

Enterprise Social Collaboration

○ Use Yammer.com service

◉ Use SharePoint Newsfeed (default)

Make Yammer the primary social experience for everyone in
your organization. Switching services will replace Newsfeed and
change the Office 365 global navigation. This update might take
up to 30 minutes for us to complete.

To learn more click here.

Figure 3-1. *Option to choose Yammer or Newsfeed for enterprise*
social collaboration

Follow these steps to set up Yammer:

1. As a global admin or SharePoint admin, log in to
   Office 365.

2. Select the app launcher icon and choose the Office
   365 Admin center. If you do not see the Office 365
   Admin center in the app launcher, this implies that
   you do not have admin rights.

3. Once you are in the Admin center, choose
   SharePoint.

4. After you choose settings, under enterprise social
   collaboration, select the Yammer.com service,
   as shown in Figure 3-1, to activate the Yammer
   conversation in SharePoint Online.

When Newsfeed is turned off, the user will experience Yammer as the
social experience where users can follow people and share information.
To avoid confusion, the feature to follow people, documents, and tags
in the SharePoint Newsfeed is turned off. If you turn Newsfeed on, you
get the features to follow people, documents, and tags in the SharePoint
Newsfeed. All data is retained, although the links to follow people,
documents, and tags are removed. Note that even when Newsfeed is off,
the SharePoint Online feature continues to work as usual and there is no

impact. Finally, whenever you create a Communication site, a Yammer feed will be present in it but you need to configure it by using the Yammer webpart:

1. Click Edit at the top right of the page.

2. Choose the Yammer webpart from the edit page.

3. If you are adding the Yammer webpart to a Team or Communication site that has an associated Yammer group, the Yammer group will be detected and added automatically. Otherwise, click Add a Group.

4. If there is no group selected, use the search bar to search for a Yammer group. See Figure 3-2.

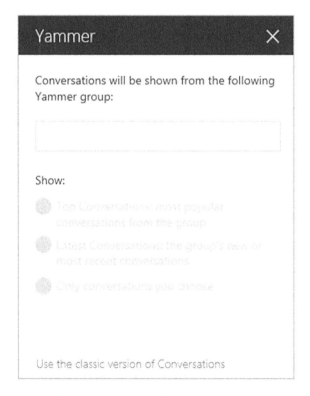

Figure 3-2. *Select Yammer groups for your site*

5. After selecting a Yammer group, select one of the following conversation options:

- **Top Conversations**—The group's most active conversations.

- **Latest Conversations**—Group conversations that are new to the reader.

- **Custom**—Select specific conversations from the Yammer group to display. This requires you to go to your chosen Yammer group, copy the URL for the conversations you want to display, and paste them into each field. You can display the Topic feed as well.

6. As you can see in Figure 3-2, click Use the Classic Version of Conversations link to see a running feed from a group, person, or topic. You can also like, reply, or view a specific conversation.

After you've published your page, you can create a new post by clicking Post a Message. You can also click a post to go directly into the Yammer group from the SharePoint page and click View More at the top-right of the webpart to see posts in that Yammer group. With Yammer conversations, you can view the most recent or most popular conversations, post new messages right from your page, and see how many likes and replies a post has.

If the SharePoint used in your organization is not SharePoint Online but is the on-premise version, you need to use Yammer Embed to embed the Yammer feed into your SharePoint on-premise. For SharePoint Server (2013 or later), you can add a Yammer feed to a SharePoint using Yammer Embed. You can add Home, Group, and My Feed into SharePoint.

Here are the steps to add the Yammer feed using Yammer Embed to an on-premise SharePoint page. In particular, we show you how to add a Yammer group using Yammer Embed to a SharePoint page.

1. In Yammer, go to the group home page that you
    want to embed into the SharePoint page. Find the
    Access Options section and select Embed this Group
    in your site. Check out Figure 3-3.

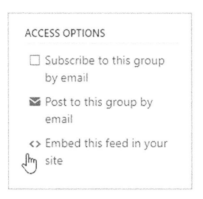

Figure 3-3. *Locate the embed feed code*

2. Click Embed This Feed in Your Site and copy the
    script from the window.

3. In your SharePoint page, click Edit and choose Web
    Part. In the Category list, select Media and Content.
    Copy the embed code in the Script Editor window
    and choose Insert. Post, save, and publish and the
    Yammer Group feed will be displayed on your page.

Attaching Files in Yammer from SharePoint

In this section we look at how we can share files from SharePoint Online
with Yammer. Due to seamless integration, the location of the host files
does not matter. When you upload a file on Yammer, it is actually hosted
in SharePoint. This is possible due to Office Groups, which is a collection
of Yammer groups, SharePoint sites, and Document Library, Planner, and
Note created for specific collaboration work. When you create a Yammer

group, there is a corresponding SharePoint Document Library, SharePoint, Planner, and OneNote site that's created. See Figure 3-4.

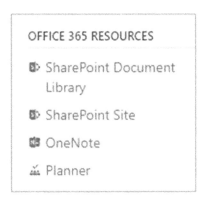

Figure 3-4. *Office 365 group*

To attach a file to a Yammer message, you can upload a file on your computer or select a file on Yammer, SharePoint, or OneDrive. At the bottom of the Yammer message, click the appropriate icon in Figure 3-5 that represents where the file is located.

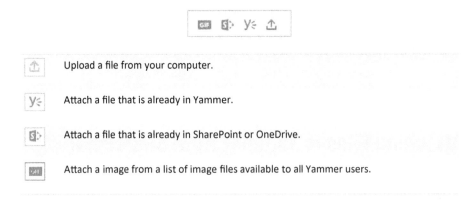

Figure 3-5. *Location of file to be uploaded into Yammer*

To upload a file from SharePoint, select the SharePoint icon ![SharePoint icon] . Then select the file you want to upload. You can find files in SharePoint in your Office 365 groups. Then select the file and post it. The file will automatically get uploaded on Yammer. See Figure 3-6.

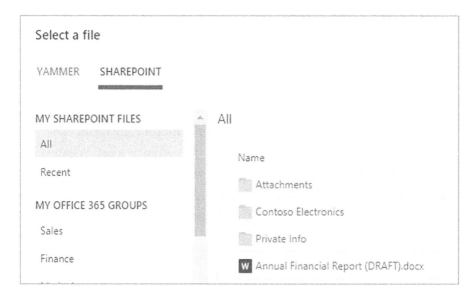

Figure 3-6. *Upload a file from SharePoint into Yammer*

Work is more than just Yammer conversations. We collaborate with our colleagues every day to create Office documents in Word, PowerPoint, and Excel. Now you can create these Office documents within Yammer. With the functionality of Office Online, you can co-author documents with colleagues, view version history, and mark important files as official. Since you're in Yammer, you can also easily share and discuss the document with your team from within your group in Yammer.

In order to help teams leverage the power of SharePoint for file storage and management, it much easier to share and discuss these files with your team on Yammer. The improved file picker lets you browse and share files from your Office 365 SharePoint Document Libraries, which means you can take advantage of SharePoint content management capabilities directly within Yammer.

SharePoint Online and Outlook Integration

In this section, we see how we can integrate SharePoint Online and Outlook to create a seamless experience for the end users. We will work with Outlook objects such as Calendars, Contacts, Emails, and Tasks and connect with SharePoint Online. These Outlook objects will appear as a SharePoint List in SharePoint Online. To view the list, you need to have Read permissions. If you have SharePoint Contributor rights, you can edit, create, and delete any Outlook objects appearing as a list. Whatever permission the user has in SharePoint, they will have that permission while working with that list in Outlook. Go to the desired SharePoint List, for example Calendar, and in the ribbon, click the Connect to Outlook button. See Figure 3-7.

Figure 3-7. *Connection to synchronize the SharePoint Calendar with Outlook*

Once you click it, a dialog box will appear to allow such connections. Once you allow it, the SharePoint Calendar will be accessible in the Outlook Calendar under Other Calendars. See Figure 3-8.

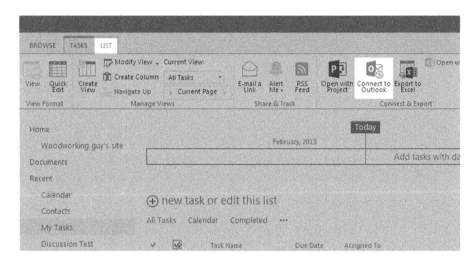

Figure 3-8. *Connection to synchronize SharePoint tasks with Outlook*

The SharePoint Connect to Outlook option also works with other SharePoint objects, such as discussion boards, libraries, and more. The Folder view in Outlook is where you see all of the SharePoint Lists and Libraries. In the Outlook Folder section, you will not only see the Calendars, Task Lists, and Contacts Lists, but any other SharePoint Lists or Libraries. The title of each connection will begin with the name of the site or subsite where the list is located, followed by the name of the particular list or library. Permissions you have on that list in SharePoint will carry over to Outlook. See Figure 3-9.

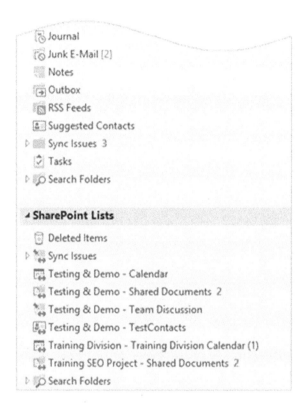

Figure 3-9. *Viewing a SharePoint List in Outlook*

Five Ways to Get Email Into a SharePoint Online Communication Site

In this section, we discover five out-of-the-box ways to upload email into SharePoint. These ways are simple and will give collaborative experience to users working with Outlook and SharePoint Online Communication sites.

Manually Save Email and Upload it Into a SharePoint Site

The first way is to do it manually. Consider email as just another file that you want to upload onto SharePoint. Follow these steps:

1. Open your email in Outlook and save it. The Outlook message format (*.msg) is recommended.

2. Go to your SharePoint site and upload this email attachment.

3. Manually save an email message to SharePoint (see Figure 3-10).

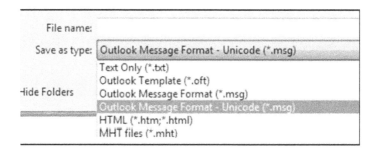

Figure 3-10. *Saving Outlook email as (*.msg)*

Send Emails to a SharePoint List or Document Library

Select SharePoint lists and libraries have unique email addresses, which you can use to send emails to lists or document libraries. This way, you can store your emails on SharePoint

Map a Drive to a SharePoint Library

Map a network drive or create a shortcut to a network location to provide access to the content of a SharePoint library. You can do this in Windows Explorer, which is similar to any directory structure on a file server. From Outlook, you can drag and drop messages into Windows Explorer and, due to the mapping in place, your emails will get uploaded onto SharePoint (see Figure 3-11).

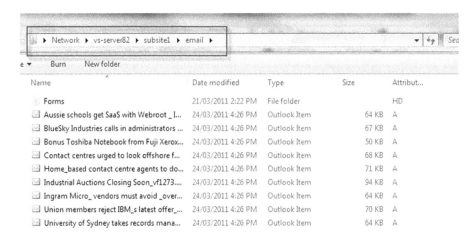

Figure 3-11. *Drag and drop attachments to Windows Explorer into the SharePoint mapped drive location*

Use the Open with Explorer Feature

In a SharePoint List or Document Library, open items using the Open with Explorer feature. Then follow the previous method (i.e., drag and drop email into the Explorer window). Your mail will then be uploaded into SharePoint (see Figure 3-12).

Figure 3-12. *Open a SharePoint List or library with the Open with Explorer option*

Use the SharePoint Discussion Board

In this case, we connect the SharePoint Discussion Board to Outlook, and then drag and drop emails into the SharePoint Discussion folder created in Outlook. Once you do this, you will have emails uploaded into the Discussion Board. Open the SharePoint Discussion Board from SharePoint and use the Connect to Outlook feature. After this, the Discussion Board will appear under the SharePoint List in Outlook, as shown in Figure 3-13. You can now drag and drop emails into the Discussion Board from within Outlook, and they will be copied across to SharePoint.

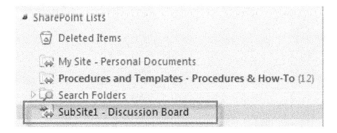

Figure 3-13. *Discussion Board in Outlook*

Summary

In this chapter, we learned how Outlook and Yammer can be integrated with SharePoint Online Communication sites to create collaborative experiences for end users. Seamless integration implies that you use one login to access different platforms, can share content between different platforms, and can use different platforms for your work. With this collaborative user experience in your pocket, you can move forward to create digital Intranets and jumpstart digital transformation.

CHAPTER 4

Create Digital Intranets

The Corporate Intranet is the key source of information for any organization. All major announcements, news, updates, and stories are communicated through the Corporate Intranet. Organizations have now become smarter and created digital Intranets, which provides an easy way to share information using graphics and multimedia, gather feedback from information consumers, and have a place for them to share information. In this chapter, we explore designing digital Intranets using the webparts available in SharePoint Communication sites.

The Background of Intranets

Intranets, as opposed to the Internet, are private networks used by organizations to communicate and engage with their employees. The Intranet is also the hub of company-related information, which is accessed by all employees of the company. With Intranets in place, information linked to different departments, organizational charts, knowledge about processes, links to other platforms, and employee-related services can be made available at your fingertips. Intranets are the organizational newspaper that provides the latest information about your organization (see Figure 4-1). Customers cannot access the Corporate Intranet; it's made only for employees.

© Charles David Waghmare 2019
C. D. Waghmare, *Beginning SharePoint Communication Sites*,
https://doi.org/10.1007/978-1-4842-4203-2_4

Intranet - An organizational newspaper		
Edition: Always latest		
Frequency: Daily Price: Free Author: Organization		
News:	Update:	Useful links
New Deals, Our company is IS27001 certified, Lauch of training centre	New CEO to visit Asian offices, Travel policy updated, lauch of new CRM system	CRM Employee database, Timesheet, Book Travel

Figure 4-1. *The Corporate Intranet is the daily organizational newspaper*

Traditionally, Intranet were maintained as a hub of information and knowledge to be made available to all employees. However, the shift has been made from traditional Intranets to digital Intranets, which are stronger versions of the Intranet. Digital Intranets are not only hubs for organizational information and knowledge, but they are also a platform to collaborate, connect, and share business related information. This shift has made been possible using modern technology.

The SharePoint platform is the most widely used for creating digital Intranets in order to create end user collaborative experience for end users. According to a Gartner report published in 2014, more than 50% of Intranets in this world are built in SharePoint. But there are other alternatives as well. Some organizations are using Drupal CMS, modern web technologies such as JavaScript, .NET, and others. Apart from digital Intranets, you also have social internets and technology such as Yammer, Jive, and SAP JAM are being used for companies using social Intranets. Facebook at work is another example of a social Intranet.

The difference between a digital and a social Intranet is not very complex. Social Intranets are identified by use of enterprise social networks such as Yammer, Jive, Chatter, and Tibbr, which are used for Intranet purposes. Digital Intranets are much stronger and you have access to rich graphical features to make Intranet pages visually appealing. Users can collaborate using information available on the digital Intranet and share additional content.

Benefits of Using an Intranet

Here are some benefits of using an Intranet:

- **Employee communication**—With an Intranet in place, it has become easy for organizations to communicate with their employees. This can be a strategic move, customer appreciation, new customer wins, leadership views and opinions, company profit and loss, organizational objectives, or links to other organizational platforms. The Intranet is also used to share knowledge so that it can create awareness and keep employees well informed. Apart from being a strategic form of communication, Intranets are used to communicate campaigns, series of weekly or biweekly communications such as about technology, and employee empowerment communications, such as awareness on pollution, eco-friendly plastic, and global warming issues. Some organizations run polls and competitions using their Intranets.

- **Communication in time**—Intranets deliver communication to employees at their convenience, which means whenever employees are in pursuit of the information, they can access it. Intranets do not send employee mass communications, as is done through email. Access to information available on the Intranet is solely in the hands of employees at their convenience. Information available on the Intranet does not distract employees when they are busy with work by sending notifications or triggering updates.

- **Improves employee productivity**—Intranets provide access to application links that are vital for employees to perform their roles and responsibilities in the organization. The Intranet has vital business information that's required by employees in their day-to-day work. For example, say you are working on a customer RFP and you need the number of SAP-based certified professionals and the quality standards achieved by your organization. This information is available on the Intranet whenever you need it. Logging in to the Intranet is simple as it usually synchronized with the corporate active directory and integrated with a sign-in mechanism. This means one single click and a one-time investment to enter the user name and password. Any employee can access the information. Any employee who is part of the organization can access the Intranet without any special access request.

- **Web publishing**—Intranets are web-based platforms that can be accessed using URLs. With a web publishing mechanism, managing cumbersome corporate knowledge has become less complex and access to it has become very easy. Using web technologies and hypermedia, employees can access organizational information such as HR policies and training videos. They can process documents and download attachments, and this become possible using technologies such as Acrobat, Flash, and inline video players.

- **Business operations and management**—Intranets are used for developing and deploying business applications. Information such as the know-how of an application, upcoming changes, and downtime information is made available on the Intranet.

- **Saves on costs**—An Intranet is a cost-saving solution and to demonstrate let's look at a couple of examples. Say your organization must train its employees in ethics and compliance and the training video is around 1GB in size. Imagine without an Intranet, every employee would be forced to download this video, consuming lots of Intranet bandwidth and local machine size. With an Intranet in place, such training videos, independent of size, can be made available. Another example is circulating employee code of conduct documents, which often undergo changes. Imagine without an Intranet in place, that the organization would be required to send each version of that document through email and employees again would be forced to download it multiple times. With an Intranet in place, you make this document available online and amend it whenever you need to.

- **Create a common culture among employees**— Information available on the Intranet is unique. All employees who are part of the organization can access the same information. Even temporary workers, subcontractors, and interns can access the Intranet so that they can become part of the same employee culture. The Intranet is an umbrella that holds employees with company information.

- **Augments collaboration**—Information and knowledge available on the Intranet is used by employees in day-to-day work and this information is shared between employees. With integration in place, news or articles on the Intranet can be shared with other platforms. For example, news articles from SharePoint can be shared with Yammer and employees can discuss and exchange ideas and generate collaboration.

- **Employee engagement**—Modern Intranets provide two-way communication by means of surveys, polls, and voting features. With such features in place, employees can react to the information shared on the Intranet. Some companies also provide discussion forum features in order for employees to discuss and provide feedback on the information made available on the Intranet.

- **Built for a unique audience**—In an organization, you have employees with experience from different backgrounds, such as Finance, Legal, Information Technology, Administration, and Human Resources. Information on the Intranet is made available in such a way that it is comprehensible to all employees with different backgrounds, experiences, and ranks.

- **Quick updates**—Information and knowledge made available on the Intranet has to undergo version changes due to business changes. After such business change, information and knowledge is updated and the most recent version is made available for end users. Modern Intranets also provide access to archive versions as well. Some communication on the Intranet is really fast. When there is heavy rainfall or snowfall and roads are blocked, the trains or metro are not functioning due to strikes and other major reasons, the Intranet helps you quickly publish such communication about these situations.

Create Visually Captivating Digital Intranets

A digital Intranet plays multiple roles in any organization. It's the place where you share information, updates, and stories about your organizations. It is the official channel to publish company related information. Intranets are also a platform to communicate with your employees and with digital Intranets, so it has become two-way communication. Such digital Intranets have become the foundation of the digital workforce and workplace. With such Intranets, people are able to voice their opinions and views and share ideas, which can help the organization be better and adapt to changes successfully. All this is captured in Figure 4-2.

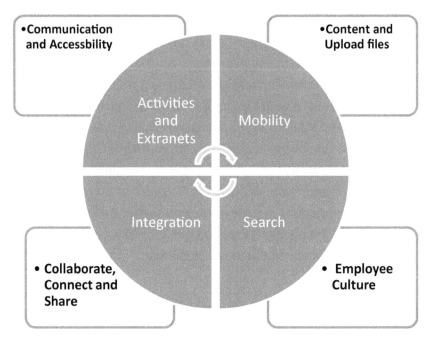

Figure 4-2. *A framework for a digital Intranet using Communication sites*

Many successful Intranets include these elements:

- **Communication and accessibility**—Communication with your employees is the key in digital Intranets, as communication is not one way but is two-way. It is social and open communication where multiple people can participate. Accessibility is also important as information must be available on the Intranet clearly and users should not get lost. To achieve this, you can create a Communication site with home pages that include news and information across the organization, overall navigation systems to different Team sites, and URLs to applications.

- **Content and upload files**—A place where different departments can make their services available to the rest of the organization. For example, departments such as Human Resources, Information Technology, Legal, and Mobility can use the Communication site to make business content available to employees. The Human Resources department can provide access to employee policies and benefits, code of conduct, business ethics, and compliance through a Communication site. The Information Technology department can display content linked to software and hardware policies, information security, and bandwidth. The Legal department can display intellectual property and Mobility can display information and rules related to business travel using a Communication site. Attachments linked to these sites should be downloaded or uploaded.

- **Collaborate, connect, and share**—This is the social aspect of a digital Intranet. Communication sites linked with Teams or Yammer provide collaborative experiences in that employees can openly share content and build connections with other users. With the Yammer webpart, integrating Yammer with a SharePoint communication is very simple.

- **Employee culture**—The Intranet helps to build a culture of unity, as the information or news published and communicated on the Intranet is considered an official channel. Communication sites help unify information from all departments to create a unique umbrella of information and help build an employee culture.

- **Mobility**—With digital Intranets in place with the help of the Communication site, they can be accessed using various mobile devices. With such features, real-time communication can be made available to users.

- **Extranets**—Digital Intranets have gone one step ahead with Communication sites, as they can be open for your external clients, suppliers, and partners with restricted access. Sharing and communicating with external parties has become simple with Communication sites.

- **Integration**—Having multiple systems and departments makes information scattered and siloed. It is necessary to consolidate them. By making Communication sites into Hub sites, you can make navigation simple.

- **Search**—You can find content from Communication sites and use the integrated search feature to yield results from Yammer and user profiles.

Create End User Experiences with Communication Sites

One of the major objectives is to create an awesome end user experience when using a digital Intranet. The word "awesome" in this context can be described as finding information over an Intranet very easily, communicating with end users simply, and reusing information available on Intranet to a business end. Let's look at some of the elements of SharePoint Communication sites that will create an awesome user experience.

Use Webparts

By using default webparts available on the SharePoint Communication sites, you are already on the path to creating an awesome user experience. Webparts are available under the Topic, Showcase, and Blank design areas. We discovered webparts available under design Topic and Showcase earlier in the chapter, so let's now look at a list of webparts available in the Communication site template:

- **Topic**
  - **Hero**—To bring focus and visual interest to your page
  - **News**—To publish eye-catching news, announcements, and updates
  - **Events**—To publish upcoming events
  - **Highlighted content**—To distinguish specific content from other content with filters

- **Showcase**
  - **Hero**—To bring focus and visual interest to your page
  - **Image Gallery**—To insert images or collections of images into the page

- **Blank**
  - **Bing maps**—To add maps to maps in pages
  - **Connectors**—To receive alerts and messages based on conditions you set
  - **Divider**—To break lines between webparts
  - **Document Library**—To manage files, i.e., to upload, download, and modify on-site

- **Embed**—To embed content from other sites

- **File Viewer**—To insert files such as Excel, PowerPoint, and PDFs into your pages

- **Group Calendar**—To insert an Office 365 group calendar

- **Kindle Instant Preview**—To share preview of a Kindle book

- **Link**—To add links to external and internal pages

- **Microsoft Forms**—To create to surveys, quizzes, and polls

- **Office 365 Video**—To display video in your Communication sites

- **People**—To add select people for contact purposes

- **Planner**—To add team actions to your page

- **PowerApps**—To add your customized apps built in the PowerApps service

- **Power BI**—To embed reports created in Power BI

- **Quick Chart**—To add simple charts to your page

- **Quick Links**—To pin items to your page for easy access

- **Site Activity**—To display recent activity on your Communication site

- **Site**—To showcase sites on a page; it will automatically show sites associated with a Hub site

- **Spacer**—To control vertical space on your page

- **Stream**—To display videos from the Microsoft stream

- **Text**—To add paragraph, tables, styles, bullets, indentations, highlights, and hyperlinks

- **Twitter**—To display tweets linked to your organization and its interests

- **Weather**—To display the current weather on your page

- **Yammer**—To create collaborative experiences for your end users

Integrate Mobile Functionality

Facilitating Intranet access through the mobile app is itself a digital transformation of the traditional Intranet, as they were originally only internal websites. Organizations are reluctant to develop a mobile option for Internet considering it is just an internal site for hosting content. But with SharePoint Online, Intranets are transformed into digital ones and you can access them through your mobile app. Engage your users through mobile devices. With SharePoint Communication sites, it is quite simple to consume and create content from mobile devices. Through mobile apps, viewing pages, creating articles, navigating, searching, and engaging in Yammer conversations are all very simple. You can download the SharePoint mobile app for Android, Windows, and iPhone.

Collaborate

Using Yammer webpart, you can add feeds from specific Yammer groups. Digital Intranets are designed in such a way that their viewers should not only read information but should be able to react, share it further, and comment on it. Brainstorming new topics in order to create content for the Intranet can be possible through Yammer engagement.

Customize

There are several things you can do to customize your SharePoint Online sites. You can change the logo, customize the theme to match the organizational brand, add useful links, edit pages, and add webparts. There is plenty of room for customization.

To create an awesome experience, organizations have implemented some innovative ideas using the webparts available inside Communication sites. Some organizations displayed football or ruby world cup score cards on their Intranets to bring maximum people to the Intranet. Internal competitions were rolled out and daily polls were hosted on the Intranet. In short, innovative techniques facilitate the use of SharePoint to create awesome experiences.

Using the Intranet, organizations have rolled out smart engines, called an integrated search engine, which gives you search results across all platforms. This was achieved by providing a user interface (UI) of a search engine on the Intranet home page. Organizations—in order to gain maximum viewers—are thinking of adding features such as shopping sites, Uber access sites, and embedded feeds linked to the company from external social media channels such as Facebook, LinkedIn, and Instagram.

Seven Steps to Building an Intranet Using SharePoint Communication Sites

In this section, we will learn about seven practical steps that you can consider when building an Intranet for your organization. An Intranet is the place where employees look for latest communication, events, updates, and announcements in order to remain updated and be efficient in their day-to-day work. Employees also look for business information, onboarding templates, and useful links to the business application. Considering this, the following steps can be used when building Intranet sites using SharePoint.

Strategy

This is most crucial step to consider when building your Intranet. We have clear objectives that we want to achieve and understand the benefits we want. Designing a strategy will help to develop clear-cut plans on how your Intranet should look, the contents, how employees are going to consume information, and how the organization can achieve business growth. Figure 4-3 shows a possible skeleton of an Intranet.

Intranet					
Announcements		Hot News		Frequently Asked Questions (FAQs)	
Corporate Communication		Weekly Series		Employee Directory	
Strategic Business Unit	Support Functions	Useful Links	Local Intranets	Top initiatives	Documents and Templates
Application Support	Human Resources	Yammer	US	Artificial Intelligence	Organizational Chart
Application Development	Finance	Finance Application	Australia	Automation	Processes
Implementation	IT	Knowledge Application	India	Cloud	Templates
Europe	Legal	Leave Management	China	APPS Development	Functional Documents
Asia	Communications	Others	Others	Others	Others
North America	Facility				
Others	Procurement				

Figure 4-3. *A working skeleton of a corporate Intranet*

This skeleton can be designed using SharePoint communications and its webparts, such as the Document Library, Events, Hero and others. Most people do not see it until they create it, but with SharePoint Communication sites, you can see the structure somewhat before it is developed. What I mean is when I think of an Intranet, I think of a Hub site. Similarly, when I think of local sites, I think of different Communication sites mapped to a unique Hub site, and when I think of useful links, I think of webparts. SharePoint Hub sites and Communication sites are explained in Chapter 2.

Use Webparts

As we saw in earlier sections, the SharePoint Communication sites include a rich list of webparts that can be used on your Intranet. The following webparts can be used to design your Intranet using SharePoint.

- **Hero**—To bring focus and visual interest to your page

- **News** —To publish eye-catching news, announcements, and updates

- **Events**—To publish upcoming events

- **Highlighted Content**—To distinguish specific content from other content with filters

- **Image Gallery**—To insert images or collections of images on a page

- **Yammer**—To create a collaborative experience for your end users

- **Document Library**—To manage files, i.e. to upload, download, and modify them on-site

- **Embed**—To embed content from other sites

- **File Viewer**—To insert files such as Excel, PowerPoints, and PDFs into your pages

- **People**—To add select people for contact purposes

- **Site Activity**—To display recent activity on your Communication site

- **Text**—To add paragraph, tables, styles, bullets, indentations, highlights, and hyperlinks

Configure Page Layouts

Making visually appealing Communication sites is very important so that your employees do not feel bored when reading information. Therefore, it is important that you use pictures and configure page layouts. Here are the available layouts:

- **Top Story**—Latest articles can be displayed on the left of your site page

- **List View**—Display articles in a single column below one another

- **Side-by-Side**—Display articles in a single column next to another

Configure Top Navigation

There could be many possibilities for the top navigation. Choose the best ones depending on your needs. Probable suggestions are Configure SBU Pages, Employee Directory, Useful Links, Policies and Procedures, and Templates. Country sites could also be your choice.

Use Pictures

As you have heard, "A picture is worth a thousand words". Use pictures whenever you want to communicate or publish information so that users get the message. Normally, Generation Y users are not used to reading large amounts of text, and providing pictures with some text is a nice way to convey your message.

Use Launchpad

Once your Intranet is ready, make it visible to the organization. Send mailers, display posters in the cafeteria or pantry where you have lots of employees, and make it the default page in your browser. The more you make it visible, the more viewers you are likely to receive.

Get User Feedback

Once the site is ready, your job is not over yet. You need to take continuous feedback from end users to make the Intranet look its best per user expectations. Most organizations, once they have the site ready, think the work is done and they do not pay attention to it. If your Intranet is created as per people's expectations, things will change and you will gain maximum participation. Engage users as part of the transform journey of the Intranet through their continuous feedback. Assign ownership for each page, define roles for content authors and editors, and make the picture library available as per the organization's copyright's policies. If you have these channels for feedback, you are heading in the right direction to have an evolving digital Intranet.

Creating your Intranet with SharePoint Communication sites can be as difficult or as easy as you make it. But when you strategize, plan, and consider user feedback, you will definitely have the Intranet that your employees want. If you have what employees want in place, you have the best-in-class.

Summary

In this chapter, you learned how to can create Intranets using SharePoint communications and explored the list of webparts that SharePoint Online allows to design Intranets. We also saw that there is extra coding required to develop Intranet sites and everything you need is available by default in the form of webparts. If we use these webparts efficiently, we can create useful Intranets.

CHAPTER 5

Integration of Communication Sites with Office 365 Services

In the previous chapter, we saw how SharePoint Communication sites can be used to create digital Intranets very simply. Further, we saw how digital Intranets using SharePoint Communication sites make communication and collaboration with end users very easy and straightforward. With the available webparts, you can create visually captivating social Intranets. In this chapter, we will look at the integration of SharePoint Communication sites with Office 365 products and discuss high-end SharePoint communications with information flowing from other Office 365 applications such as Yammer, Power BI, Teams, Stream, and others. In the beginning, we look at the Office 365 product family and discuss its integration into SharePoint Online.

© Charles David Waghmare 2019
C. D. Waghmare, *Beginning SharePoint Communication Sites*,
https://doi.org/10.1007/978-1-4842-4203-2_5

An Introduction to Office 365

Office 365 is a family of products and services hosted in the cloud and operated in a Software as a Service (SaaS) model. Office 365 services include Office Online, SharePoint Online, Exchange Online, OneDrive, Yammer, Teams, Stream, Sway, OneNote, Publisher, Skype (to be integrated into Teams), Delve, Planner, Project, and Visio. The list of services may change by the time you read this, as some are removed or integrated into others. Due to user expectations and the Microsoft roadmap, Office 365 services are dynamic in nature. New releases are deployed almost every month, changes are announced to meet user expectations, unused features are deprecated following user feedback, and beta testing of new features happens frequently. It's all happening with Microsoft. Microsoft also helps customers deploy Office 365 in their organization and get the full benefits. Microsoft has a team of technical account managers who help customers move from on-premise platforms to the cloud.

Office 365 services are hosted in the cloud and, by using the Internet, users access these services. The cloud has been a game changer, as it transforms how applications are managed. Let's look at what the cloud is and see how this big transformation has happened because of cloud technology.

Earlier organizations hosted their servers in the office building or on nearby premises. To manage those servers, datacenters were built by organizations and, to manage them, there were hardware, monitoring, and networking teams to ensure that the servers were up and running 24X7 or per service level agreements with customers. There were situations where incidents linked to business applications were traced to hardware or network problems as their root causes. Hardware migrations, such as servers, memory upgrades, and maintenance activities, were some of the regular and everlasting activities that organizations were required to perform. In addition to technical activities, there were security and data privacy activities that impacted the IT infrastructure. Organizations were required to deal with infrastructure issues along with core business issues. Some companies outsourced such activities in order to focus on their core business.

Infrastructure management also required a help desk to manage operations effectively. Help desk teams were comprised of Level 1, Level 2, and Level 3 teams in order to provide sufficient support to their end users. Quality management of infrastructure also played a key role in achieving standardizations, such as SAAS 70, ISO27001, and others.

With such an investment in hardware, software, processes, and manpower in infrastructure management, this lead to loss even though organizations did not deal in the infrastructure business.

So, how has the cloud technology helped in this regard? If the infrastructure so far is managed by a specialized organization and the core organizations continue to focus on the business, this will allow the organization to sell its services and products in a better way with defined business goals and not have to worry about the infrastructure. This is the start of the digital transformation in any organization. In addition to this, product companies also realized that their customers were not interested in buying on-premise products, therefore, they changed their business model and started building cloud solutions. These cloud solutions are operated through a Software as a Service model, which means that customers only pay for usage and don't have to worry about managing updates or dealing with size limitations. They just pay and use the service as needed.

Benefits of the Cloud Technology

Companies used to manage the infrastructure for email exchange and Office products (which included organization-wide installation, upgrades, and support). They also had to host, manage, and upgrade other Microsoft applications such as SharePoint, Skype, and others. But with Office 365, everything has moved to the cloud. Today, organizations buy an Office 365 subscription and start using the services—such as Microsoft Office, Corporate Active Directory, and others. They do not have to invest time and money on installation, support, and maintenance. The following sections discuss some of the benefits of the cloud technology.

Savings

If an organization is worried about the price of the cloud technology, they have to be serious about the decision because there is an initial investment. However, once that initial investment is made, there is zero operating cost. Before implementing a cloud technology, organizations have to define their Return on Investment (ROI) so that the benefits are realized. Once an organization is on the cloud, accessing data is easy. There will be no cost for infrastructure management and there will be enhanced business focus. Organizations are required to pay to use services and, apart from this, they are no challenges for them. Most cloud infrastructure service providers assure 99% availability and they maintain the disaster recovery and business continuity plans. Therefore, organizations do not have to worry about what will happen when the infrastructure is down.

Security

Today, security is very important and organizations do not want to take in data leaks. Organizations, when they host their information in the cloud, have several concerns of data getting leaked, thus causing potential threats to the organization. However, could service providers have surveillance across datacenters and monitoring and alerts are in place to signal any issues. In reality, cloud services are able to achieve information security related measurements more effectively, as this is one of their core business tenants and central scope of work. But organizations that have distributed

IT work their distributed team and information is just one part of the plan. One report published by Dell Inc. reported that companies that invest in big data, cloud, and security enjoy up to 53 percent faster revenue growth than their competitors.

Useful for Startups

Small organizations, startups, and home-based organizations struggle to manage and protect their own datacenters. Having a cloud technology in place, such organizations can easily manage their content and collaborate with colleagues. In today's world, if you need to start a home business, hosting a website, configuring a mail domain, and communicating with clients becomes easy as the result of cloud services. With such a transformation, many small sized companies are able to build their websites, engage in communication with clients, and improve the quality of products and service. Not only using websites, small-scale organizations now also have mobile apps in place in order to engage customers using their mobile devices. Cloud service providers provide plenty of opportunities in the market for small businesses and more and more startups, small organizations, and home business are choosing the cloud option.

Flexibility

The ability to quickly meet business demands was one of the most important reasons a business decided to move to a cloud environment. This was the sentiment of 65 percent of respondents to an InformationWeek survey. The business situation in today's world is very dynamic and sometimes we get customer requests to install a business application and make it accessible in one day. This is close to impossible, as to procure hardware with internal financial norms takes time and setting up the infrastructure will take even more time. In a cloud situation, you can provide your services in the form of SaaS and provide your applications to multiple new customers every day. The job of providing a solution to dynamic business needs from clients has become difficult primarily because business focus on infrastructure is secondary as compared to core business functions. Hence, business flexibility is very limited within the internal infrastructure team. Hence, to remain flexible in business environments, customers are moving to cloud-based partnerships.

Mobility

A cloud service provider can provide access to corporate assets through mobile devices. Some organizations have launched an initiative called Bring Your Own Device (BYOD), which means that employees can use their personal desktop, laptop, or mobile device to access corporate data and get their business activities done. Organizations have given their employees corporate mobile phones or email access using mobile devices so that employees can remain connected and can collaborate in times of crises. Companies are spending more money creating visually friendly mobile apps to engage customers through mobile devices. An organization that has a cloud partnership will definitely have ample business challenges managing mobile apps for their end customers. Cloud service providers are aligned with this ongoing business trend.

Insights

Once you have data in the cloud, there is a huge number of transactions with stored data. Along with your employees, your clients will perform a huge number of transactions with that data. You just cannot imagine the number of transactions that a social media organization or banking organization experiences as they create room to analyze data and create insights.

Facebook, for example, has millions of users, posts, and images and this increases day-by-day, creating a huge amount of data transactions. Today, Internet banking and mobile banking is the norm and people rely on these two mediums to manage their finances. As a result, there is a huge amount of transactions taking place on banking data. Cloud service providers are often integrated into business intelligence to provide statuses of this data and plan actions accordingly. Some organizations connect their internal social media applications such as Yammer or Jive to business intelligent platforms to understand the sentiments of the network, whether it's good or bad.

Employee Collaboration

Global organizations have a presence all over the world, in cities and countries everywhere. For such an organization to function, small units based out of different countries must be able to collaborate effectively. The company's business goals are shared with these small units and executing them requires employee collaboration. With the help of cloud platforms, employees can collaborate, connect, and share information on business-related activities. Today, almost all collaboration platforms such as Yammer, Tibbr, Salesforce, Chatter, and Jive are available as SaaS. The on-premise platform, on the other hand, posed plenty of challenges to employee collaboration. One of the obvious reasons was the requirement of a dedicated infrastructure and workforce to support the on-premise platform.

Quality Control

Organizations that rely on cloud service providers to host information are in a controlled situation when it comes to the quality of that data. Generally, in a siloed organization, information shared by employees is scattered, which can produce different versions. Searching for such information is a painful task for any employee in the organization. When you have your data hosted in the cloud, information is stored once and there are no different versions. Using a search engine, employees can access information easily. For example, in a cloud-based Office 365 program, when you upload a document in Yammer, it is stored in SharePoint, which is ideally a content management system. Documents uploaded from Yammer can be shared with SharePoint sites and vice versa. This is indeed a very good example of how two cloud-based platforms seamlessly integrate with each other and can produce a unique experience for the end users.

Data Privacy

When cloud service providers reside outside of your country, a list of challenges around data privacy can arise. For example, European data privacy laws do not allow data belonging to European countries to be hosted outside of European boundaries. The law identifies the risk in data leakage of personal data of European Union users. Similarly, the German workers council does not approve of using cloud services hosted outside of European boundaries. With such laws, there have been many datacenters built in Europe so that such laws are carefully followed and there is no leakage of personal data of European users. Today, managing an infrastructure using the cloud has become simple and you can choose the region in which you want to host the server. For example, in Microsoft Azure, you can choose Europe, Asia, United States of America, or Australia as the region to host your data.

Disaster Recovery

VMware published a survey result in which 43 percent of IT executives said they plan to invest in or improve cloud-based disaster recovery solutions. Disasters are unpredictable, but you need to get back in control of the situation as quickly as possible.

When I started my career, I was working as a database administrator for a bunch of European clients. Application and infrastructure support was managed by our team. With such a mixture of teams who were proving end-to-end services, clients suffered during disaster recovery. There were situations where, due to heavy rainfall, an infrastructure capacity issue, or an application bug, we were unable to provide support and the servers remained unavailable for 2-3 days. We had to provide lots of communications to the end users and provide them with status update.

When I started working on Yammer, which is SaaS, I did not experience downtime that lasted for more than one hour. There was scheduled downtime for maintenance activities, which was okay. But unscheduled downtime that went on for more than an hour just didn't happen. When I visited the success center to check out the application status, I could see some failures that were easily fixed by Microsoft without having any impact on the end users. Cloud service providers manage your disaster recovery with an assurance of 99.99% uptime.

Preventing Data Loss

As mentioned earlier, organizations that are using on-premise versions of data cannot store them in a common location and, as a result, multiple versions are often created. To worsen this problem, end users do not get the correct information when they search for content. In addition to these problems, there are situations such as employees losing their laptops or hard drives that become corrupted. In those cases, there are often no backup systems in place for all types of data storage. Some organizations do not back certain types of data in order to conserve space. In such a scenario, there is a high possibility that your data is lost and cannot be recovered. The cloud solution always offers data backups and zero data loss. They include specialized monitoring tools and applications to prevent data loss. When you sign an agreement with a cloud service provider, they will agree to 99.99% data loss prevention.

Automatic Software Updates

As we know, software and server updates can be frustrating when they pop up when we are working on a crucial task. Deploying software updates is a painful task, as the deployment team has to install these updates at a central server and from there they are triggered to the end users' machines. Further, organizations have to send communications about the software update. Sometimes, due to incompatible machine configurations, such updates are not successful. Therefore, the deployment team has to manage incidents with respect to this issue. With the cloud solution, this situation is much more friendly. Automatic updates are triggered when you log in to your machine or they happen automatically when you are working. And in many cases, you do not have to restart your machine after the update.

Competitive Edge

Organizations that use a cloud solution and those that prefer on-premise solutions are depending on their individual business strategy and plans to become more competitive than their customers. A recent Verizon study showed that 77 percent of businesses feel that the cloud technology gives them a competitive advantage, and 16 percent believe this advantage is significant. If organizations delay in choosing the cloud solution, they lag behind in competitiveness as their customers move forward. By the time they choose a cloud solution, the race may already be won by their competitors.

Sustainability

Organizations need to address waste at each level. Hosting in the cloud has been found to be more sustainable and results in a smaller carbon footprint. The Pike Research report predicted that datacenter energy consumption is likely to drop by 31 percent from 2010 to 2020 based on the adoption of cloud solutions and other virtual data options.

This benefit of the cloud solution is experienced by end users today and this is evident in the strategy followed called *cloud first*. When an on-premise structure is moved to the cloud, the business enjoys more effective ways of working. Office 365 has all the benefits we described. Adoption of Office 365 is more efficient and Microsoft has made efforts to offer their services in a better, richer, and friendly way.

Integrating SharePoint Communication Sites with the Office 365 Products

As mentioned in the beginning of the chapter, Office 365 is a family of products that are seamlessly integrated. With one login credential, you can access all the services and all the content can be shared within these services. In this section, we discuss will how SharePoint Online can be integrated with the Office 365 services such as OneNote, OneDrive, Teams, and Stream.

SharePoint Communication Sites with OneNote

When you are in a meeting, a workshop, or a conference, OneNote is the best option to take notes, which you can then use to create content. You can add images, diagrams, audio, and video in OneNote. Instead of handwritten notes, OneNote can be used to take digital notes. Using OneNote, your team will all have access to the notes for brainstorming and further actions. Integrating SharePoint Communication sites and OneNote has become easy with the OneNote app in the SharePoint library. OneNote is available in the Document Library of the Communication sites.

Use these steps in SharePoint Communication sites to integrate with
OneNote:

1. To open a notebook in a SharePoint Communication
   site, click the icon associated with the OneNote
   webpart in the Communication site to add your
   notes. See Figure 5-1.

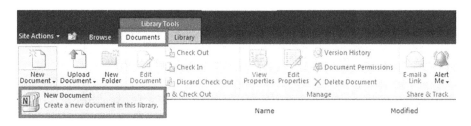

Figure 5-1. *Open a notebook in OneNote*

2. You can also open a notebook in OneNote by using
   the Open link on the Home tab. The OneNote app
   automatically saves your changes to the SharePoint
   site, as shown in Figure 5-2.

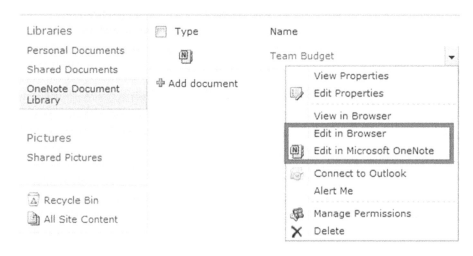

Figure 5-2. *Edit a notebook directly in OneNote*

3. Click the link associated with the notebook in
    OneNote and copy the URL from the web browser.
    This URL can be shared through email, a Team site,
    and Skype.

4. To edit a notebook, click Edit in the browser.
    Multiple users can edit one notebook in OneNote.
    Further, you can track changes of who is contributing
    to which piece of content by clicking the Show
    Authors option available in OneNote. See Figure 5-3.

***Figure 5-3.** Show Authors and version history of Notebook*

5. To keep track of who is contributing which pieces
    of content, click the View tab, and then click Show
    Authors. You can also view versions of the notebook.
    Also, you can manage permissions for the notebook
    by inheriting permissions from the Document
    Library or by creating new permissions, which are
    managed by the SharePoint Admin.

SharePoint Communication Sites and OneDrive for Business

Using OneDrive, you can store files from your machine on the cloud and access them whenever you want from any device. You can share them with people within the organization and outside the organization. As part of Office 365, OneDrive allows you to update your files and share them from any part of world. This includes Microsoft office documents as well.

A SharePoint Communication site is a place where users can collaborate and communicate using files, documents, and ideas. It is a place to facilitate two-way communications between different teams and departments. SharePoint Communication sites offer features such as document libraries, task lists, calendars, workflows, wikis, and other features to help your team communicate and collaborate.

Office 365 SharePoint Online and OneDrive store your files and documents in the cloud. You can sync them from SharePoint to OneDrive and vice versa. As a SharePoint admin, you are required to synchronize the SharePoint Online sites using OneDrive. Follow these steps to do so:

1. Sign in to Office 365 as a global admin or SharePoint admin.

2. From the app launcher icon in Office 365 in the upper-left, choose Admin to open the Office 365 Admin center. Choose SharePoint under Admin center and click Settings.

3. Ensure that the OneDrive Sync Button is set to Show the Sync Button, as shown in Figure 5-4.

OneDrive Sync Button

Show the Sync button in OneDrive to help users install and set up the new sync client.

◉ Show the Sync button
○ Hide the Sync button

Figure 5-4. *Show the OneDrive Sync button*

4. To sync SharePoint files with your new client, you must also sync OneDrive files with the client. Select Start the New Client for the Sync Client for SharePoint option, as shown in Figure 5-5.

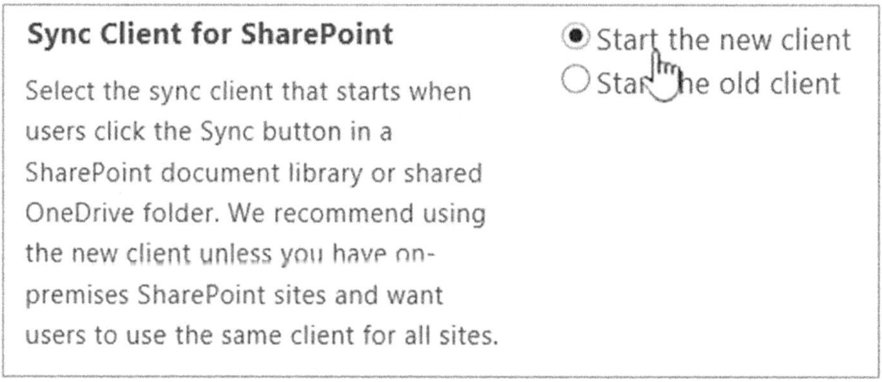

Sync Client for SharePoint

Select the sync client that starts when users click the Sync button in a SharePoint document library or shared OneDrive folder. We recommend using the new client unless you have on-premises SharePoint sites and want users to use the same client for all sites.

◉ Start the new client
○ Start the old client

Figure 5-5. *Sync client for SharePoint*

5. Click OK to save the changes.

Follow these steps to sync documents from SharePoint to OneDrive:

1. Go to the SharePoint Communication sites and head toward the Document Library.

2. Select the Documents option in the Document Library and click Sync Files with OneDrive, as shown in Figure 5-6.

Figure 5-6. *Select the Sync button*

3. After this, you will see an option to sync all the files from the site's documents, or you can select the folders you want. Follow the wizard to complete the sync process.

Microsoft Teams and SharePoint Communication Sites

For each Team site in Microsoft Teams, there is a site in SharePoint Online. Each Team site also gets a default Document Library in the default site in SharePoint to manage documents. Files shared in the Team site are automatically updated in the SharePoint Document Library and the file security options set in SharePoint are automatically reflected within Teams. Private chats in the Team site are stored in the sender's OneDrive for business.

For every Team site, a SharePoint site is created. As shown in Figure 5-7, the Shared Documents folder is the default folder created. Each channel, including the General channel (the default channel for each Team site), has a folder in Shared Documents.

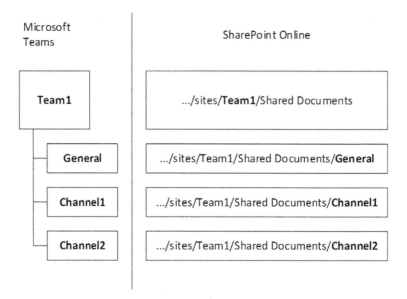

Figure 5-7. *SharePoint and Teams integration*

Flow and SharePoint Communication Sites

Microsoft Flows is an Office 365 service used to automate workflows with certain conditions. Such flows are used to automate business processes. For example, it will trigger an email when a document is added in the SharePoint Document Library or when a new lead is added to the CRM system. Follow these steps to create a flow for a list or library in SharePoint Online.

1. In a SharePoint Communication site, navigate to a list or Document Library. The Flow button will be available in the command bar of the SharePoint lists and document libraries. In SharePoint Online, the option to create a flow will only be available for site members who can add and edit items. Click Flow to create a flow, as shown in Figure 5-8.

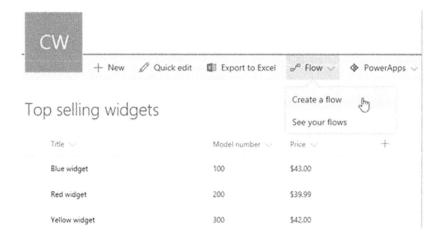

Figure 5-8. *Create a flow*

2. Once you choose Create a Flow, a list of templates
   containing default workflows will pop up on your
   screen. Some of the common workflows are Send a
   Customized Email When a New SharePoint List Item
   Is Added, Send Approval Email When New Item Is
   Added in SharePoint, When a Message Is Created in
   Yammer, Create a SharePoint List Item, and others.
   For the flow template, there are two Office 365
   services involved. The custom flow option also exists
   at the bottom of the list of templates. See Figure 5-9.

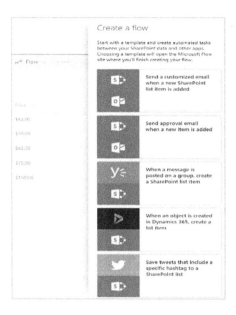

Figure 5-9. *List of templates containing default workflows*

3. In the Microsoft Flow designer, the first action displayed, which is known as a trigger, will determine how the flow will be started. More actions may be added and each new action will be dependent on the previous action. Office 365 services involved in the flow are dependent on each other. For example, if an email notification is triggered when a new item is added or updated to a SharePoint list, the Outlook and SharePoint services are dependent on each other. No service can function independently in a flow. Also there is a trigger to make the flow automatic or manual. In Figure 5-10, you can modify the standing instructions given to the flow during the initial stage.

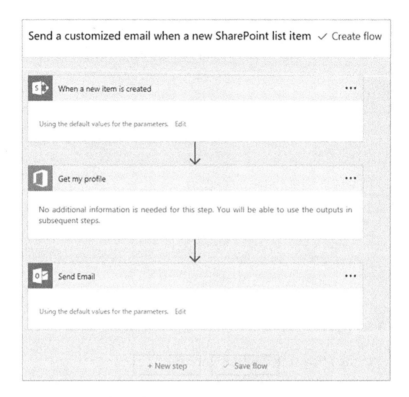

Figure 5-10. *Modify a Flow*

Stream and SharePoint Communication Sites

Microsoft Stream is an Office 365 service. It's a new video service that uses the power of enterprise video to enable knowledge sharing and easy communication. It is a platform to host all videos. It is the successor to Office 365 videos. Follow these steps to add a Microsoft Stream webpart to a SharePoint Communication site:

1. Edit the Communication site where you want to add the video and choose the plus sign to add the Stream webpart, as shown in Figure 5-11.

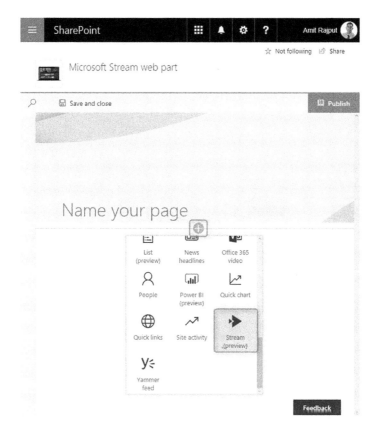

Figure 5-11. *Add the Stream webpart*

2. Choose webpart and add a video URL. Click
   the Publish button to display the stream.
   See Figure 5-12.

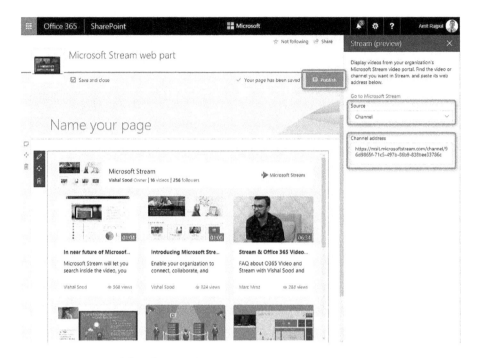

Figure 5-12. *Add video to Stream*

Summary

In this chapter, you were introduced to Office 365 and the cloud, and you learned about their benefits. Further, you learned about seamless integration of SharePoint Communication sites with OneNote, OneDrive, Teams, Flow, and Stream. Office Online is integrated into SharePoint Online, which means that you create, store, and modify Office documents in Communication sites and that you can download them to your local machine. Integration of SharePoint Communication sites with Yammer and Outlook will be discussed in the next chapter.

CHAPTER 6

Use Communication Sites to Manage Communities of Practice (CoP)

In the previous chapter, we saw how we can enhance collaboration by integrating it with Office services such as Teams, Streams, Yammer, and others. This is collaboration at its best because it's seamless. You can access the platforms with one sign-in, i.e. the Office 365 SIGNIN mechanism, and discover a unique seamless experience. In this chapter, we are going to learn how SharePoint Communication sites are used to manage multiple communities in order to create a bigger collaborative experience and build a community of practice.

Communities of Practice (CoP)

In this section, we will learn what a Community of Practice (CoP) is, including its benefits, and how we can roll out a CoP initiative using Communication sites to offer a collaborative experience. See Figure 6-1.

© Charles David Waghmare 2019

C. D. Waghmare, *Beginning SharePoint Communication Sites*,

https://doi.org/10.1007/978-1-4842-4203-2_6

Figure 6-1. A community of practice. Image from
https://unsplash.com/search/photos/community

A CoP is a group of two or more people who share common interests, issues, goals, and objectives. The group can organically evolve because of the members common interest in the area, or it is created with the objective of gaining knowledge related to a field. As a consequence of sharing information and experiences with the group, the members learn from each other and produce an opportunity to develop themselves personally and professionally.

A very well known example of communities of practice is the Xerox organization. Customer service representatives traveled door-to-door to repair and maintain Xerox machines and bring business value to the organization. During lunch or breakfast, customer service representatives shared their experience with each other and learned from each other. Further, they were able to implement these lessons in their services. Xerox as an organization found value in these interactions and created a database to share lessons, experience, and best practices. It also awarded customer service awards for their contributions. Door-to-door experience gained by customer representatives was logged in to the global platform, where it could be accessed by thousands of global customer service representatives and saved the company about 100 million USD.

Difference Between Organization Structure and CoP

Figure 6-2 shows the operating model of an organization based on departmental hierarchies.

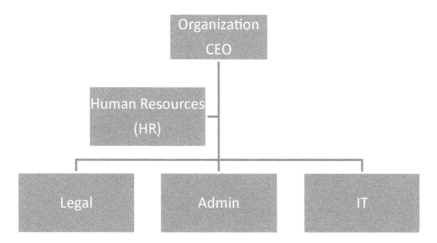

Figure 6-2. *A structured department working in a hierarchical model*

Figure 6-3 in contrast shows a typical CoP structure.

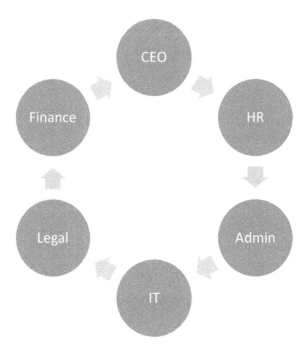

Figure 6-3. *A unstructured department working in the CoP model to create a collaborative experience*

Any company or organization is usually divided into structured groups or departments and each such department has a certain number of people in it, a defined hierarchy, departmental rules and regulations, a culture, and decision-making priorities aligned to organizational objectives. Cross-departmental organization interaction is minimal, as when needed and based on approval and conditions. Knowledge within such structured departments is captured and spread in a very structured way. People working in such departments are under some pressure but everyone has to follow departmental rules and regulations for the benefit of the organization.

An organization that has a CoP structure works a little differently. What makes such an organization different is that communities that are departments are free to collaborate, connect, and share openly to work toward a business problem. Knowledge is shared across all communities so that the benefit is reaped by all communities. Working in a community is allowed and you can openly collaborate on issues, find experts, gain insights, share content, conduct training or knowledge sharing sessions, and do plenty of other stuff. In an organization based on CoP, each member lives in a social and collaborative environment.

In this example, we saw a departmental organization turn into a CoP based organization through the discussion of customer service representatives over breakfast or lunch. Microsoft as an organization also works in a CoP manner to complete its projects. As an example, say that Microsoft wants to develop a new webpart in the SharePoint Communication sites so that its employees can book Uber rides. In this project, there are different teams or CoPs, such as the SharePoint development team, the Azure active directory team which ensures that users book rides from Active Directory, the Infrastructure team that hosts this webpart in the cloud, the Marketing team that markets and announces the feature, and the customer service managers that help customers using this webpart. So you have people from different communities or departments, with various expertise and backgrounds and different locations, but with one objective.

Benefits of Communities of Practices (CoP)

Here are some benefits of CoP.

Win new customers:

- Develop a transition and transformation approach as a key differentiator

- Provide experienced, mentor managers to the sales process

- Minimize the cost impact of transitions in the pricing

- Share best practices from existing engagements

- Develop current customers toward reference customers

- Identify and develop cross/upselling opportunities

- Position solution design as the enabler of high-quality services

- Adapt standard solution design to specific customer needs

- Solution design is the basis for competitive pricing

Drive standardization:

- Use a common, proven approach for the transition for all proposals

- Accelerate the transition and minimize costs

- Provide reusable for processes, tools, and templates

- Ensure the usage of the standard methods and tools

- Extend the utilization of the production centers and their capabilities

- Ensure consistent standard delivery structure for all customers

- Ensure usage of standard methods and tools

Better collaboration:

- Ensure quick staffing of transition roles

- Make best use of existing knowledge and assets

- Promote new roles as an attractive career path

- Provision/exchange templates and best practices
- Coach junior teammates or interns
- Cooperation with expert sales team
- Make use of best practice delivery approach
- Ensure ability to deliver

Quality in everything:

- Develop ambitious but realistic transition plans
- Ensure comprehensive risk/mitigation plans
- Drive the continuous improvement of our transition/transformation approach
- Share lessons learned and results
- Drive the continuous improvement process
- Improve customer satisfaction
- Make use of best practice delivery approach
- Ensure ability to deliver

CoP is an initiative that deals with people and is meant for them. It is designed toward growth of an organization when growth of employees is achieved. CoP is a forum where everybody will have their say over ongoing business issues or changes taking place in the organization. Management will have some work with the CoP system, as they have to constantly motivate their community so that it does not lose interest, become unfocused, and die out. Community sponsors have also their role cut out in order to meet community requirements. In my experience, I had an opportunity to implement a CoP initiative for an organization specializing in IT services and had the strength of 3,000-odd people divided into 15 different communities.

Organizations have to envision communities as an important platform to nurture talent in their current and potential areas of competitive advantage. Therefore, you must actively promote and support the CoPs as learning platforms for employees to collaborate by sharing knowledge and imparting skills.

TechnoWeb 2.0

There were two platforms used in the CoP initiative—TechnoWeb 2.0 and SharePoint. We will discuss SharePoint in more detail, but let's take a look at TechnoWeb first.

TechnoWeb 2.0 is a Yammer-like enterprise social networking platform created by an organization for its employees. TechnoWeb contained plenty of networks (in Yammer we call them groups) to share knowledge. Employees create networks and join or ask for specific expertise. People with common domain knowledge are grouped. Networks dynamically aggregate content and create clusters. Experts can identify their peers. Unplanned communication can be stimulated, i.e., all companywide announcements. Its features were activity stream micro-blogging, integration of external content, such as blogs, wikis, rating thanking, and advanced tagging. TechnoWeb 2.0 differs from other social platforms as it was built around networks focused on knowledge areas unlike object-centered networks like YouTube, Flickr, or Wikis and person-centered around LinkedIn or Xing. Here were the benefits of TechnoWeb:

- Exchange of information and knowledge so as to identify cross-sector competences and leverage synergies and innovation potential in an integrated technology corporation.

- Facilitated voluntary and direct knowledge sharing between experts.

- Dynamic structure of content and know-how.

- Cross-linkage to existing contents and tools (e.g. blogs, wikis, SharePoint, etc.).

- Very low entrance barrier to create own technology network (open platform).

- Based on Web2.0 features as experienced in existing social networks.

- No cost for users.

- What is not intended: Creation of a new database for technologies.

Here is the framework for the CoP initiative that the community was asked to follow:

- Build a community objective

- Fill and circulate a GAA community survey

- Create a community on TechnoWeb and add members to it

- Upload your plans and documents on the community page

- Create new ideas under the Submit Your Ideas link

- Send updated status tracker of activities for governance

The following is a list of engagement activities which each community was expected to perform in order to meet the CoP objectives.

- List of network members mentioning hub and spoke (regional/cluster)

- Develop a community plan covering scope, goals/objectives, defined output, and other knowledge resources and active members

- Propose an investment plan with ideas

- Create TechnoWeb communities

- Respond to community surveys

- Integrate or migrate content from existing community sites to new destinations, post validation

- Provide a communication pack on what CoP is and other introductory material

A community survey was rolled out under membership expectations. Here is the feedback from the community members. A full 62 percent of the community members were able to participate in the survey:

- 75% of respondents said that the CoP initiative will help them collaborate with peers and colleagues based on different locations and countries

- 62% of respondents said that there must be support from community leaders for the growth of community

- 60% of respondents said that they do not want reply mails as it consumes too much time.

- 70% of respondents said that the CoP initiative will help them problem solve, gain customer satisfaction, follow standardized processes, and share knowledge.

These results show that even before the initiative was started, members agreed the objective behind this survey by answering it positively. Weekly meetings were conducted by the community sponsor with the community leads to discuss progress and challenges. Minutes from these weekly meetings were shared with the CEO for his feedback and comments. Here are the accomplishments of this initiative:

- Total membership of 3,000 members was achieved

- Workshops and internal offering presentations, documentations, and solution to problems were shared across various TechnoWeb networks by different community members

- Customer appreciation was shared through TechnoWeb

- Community charters, plans, and required engagement lists were uploaded on the SharePoint page

- SharePoint sites became a unique place for a document repository

- Events were organized through TechnoWeb and training documents were hosted on the SharePoint site

CoP does look very complex when you just look at the concept, but when you implement it, it becomes simple and valuable to your career, the employees, and the organization. This implementation of CoP, I did some eight years ago, at the time of writing this book, but it is still close to my heart.

CoP Using SharePoint Communication Sites

In this section, we discover the manner in which we can implement the CoP initiative using SharePoint Communication sites. Today, it has become quite simple to drive such initiatives using modern features of Communication sites, as we have observed in previous chapters. No customized development is needed unless you have a very specific purpose. Using Communication sites, each community can be managed with ease and this can be done by creating different Communication sites over a single Hub site. Consider the following steps when executing CoP through Communication sites.

Identify the Purpose of CoP Initiative

Before doing anything, identify why you want to have a CoP initiative in your organization. Possible reasons could be to make your employees be collaborative by sharing work-related problems and solutions. You want to make your organization social by adopting a people-first direction. You want to reduce the gap between employees and management. You want to make your organization a place of knowledge sharing. You want to go digital with the CoP initiative. Conduct a YamJam session on Yammer with your employees and crowd-source the objective for your CoP.

In the previous example, we saw that knowledge sharing was the criteria to create a CoP using TechnoWeb and SharePoint. Once you set up an objective or purpose, it becomes clear to you what goals you want to achieve and what you must do to achieve these goals. There should clarity in such initiatives on a day-to-day basis. You'll need to deal with people and imagine if your objective had some ambiguity—employees will not cooperate as they themselves would be in difficult position. So it is important that you define a clear purpose or objective for the CoP initiative with the help of the employees and management.

Identify the Communities

Once the purpose is clear, it is time to identify the communities. The organization can be divided into communities that are somewhat like departments, but with different backgrounds. You can have communities based on the standard organization structure such as Human Resources, Information Technology, Legal, Logistics, and Operations. Or, you can have communities based on the kind of work you do. For example, if you are on the Application Services Management (AMS) aspect of an IT industry, a set of communities in that area could be Change Management, Incident Management, and Problem and Procurement Management. This is subjective and entirely depends on the owner of the CoP program what types of communities are required, how they should work, and their expectations. So taking these aspects into consideration, communities can be created.

In Communication sites, you can create one Hub site for organizational related matter and all the communities can be connected to this Hub site. By having such a structure, each community will have rights to manage their site and decide on their own. Any change made will not impact the Hub site and it will work as usual. So you can make different community sites using SharePoint Communication sites. Once the list of communities is approved, the next step is to create sites for them with the standard layout across all communities. See Figure 6-4.

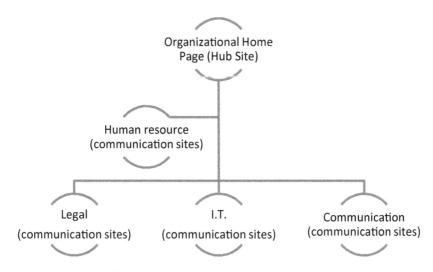

Figure 6-4. List of communities for CoP

For a community site in CoP, you play with webparts to make it visually appealing. Create a strong home page using the Hero and Story webparts. Make the site collaborative by adding the Yammer webpart. Add customized apps using PowerApps. Add a Document Library to create a repository of documents. With such an approach, any site can be redeveloped at any given point in time without affecting other sites.

Define the Community Roles

Once you define the communities you want to have in your CoP initiative, you need to define the roles that you want to have. We are not going to define a hierarchy like the one we have in a traditional organization, but by defining roles, we are going to define the responsibility of each part of the community organization. Once this is clear, people will know what they need to do and there will not be any ambiguity.

Responsibilities will be simple and each individual will clearly know what contributions are required from their side to achieve the community objective and further their own career path. In an organization based on the CoP way of working, corporate growth depends on the growth of the people, so people need to be clear about their contribution, as it will impact the company's growth. On the contrary, if the organization is lagging, that means the associated communities are growing up to the mark and some changes are needed. Figure 6-5 shows one example of the community structure in a CoP initiative.

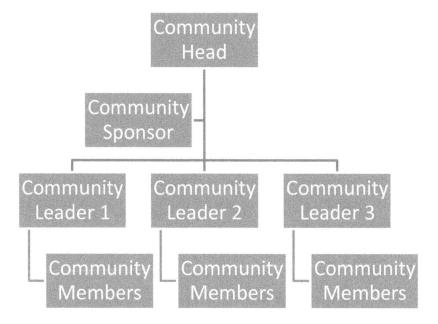

Figure 6-5. *Community roles*

We'll look in detail at these roles and responsibilities in the following sections.

Community Head

The head of the community overall is responsible and accountable for the CoP initiative. Heads will have to make sure that the initiative runs smoothly and mitigates major challenges. Heads will have to ensure that the spirit of the community is always good and if there is some major deviation, action will be required. The head is also responsible for ensuring that the community's financial targets are met, tangible business value is generated, and that they are answerable to stakeholders.

Community Sponsor

The community sponsor reports to the head. The sponsor will allocate budget to different communities to make sure the community objectives are achieved. The sponsor will also need to review progress and assess challenges and obstacles in the CoP initiative. The sponsor owns the governance part. The sponsor will need to meet with community leaders on a weekly basis to track status and report to the head of the community. The community sponsor will appoint community leaders based on their areas of expertise. The sponsor is crucial, as this is the middle level between the community head and the leaders.

Community Leader

A community leader is expected to be an expert in an area that the community objectives define. If you have community based on SharePoint, a community leader would be expected to be an expert in SharePoint so that there is a clear understanding of the community objectives and value it will generate to the organization. Also, the community leader provides guidance to the community members, identifies area of opportunities, and ensures smooth execution of the community engagement activities. The community leader role can be compared to a coach or mentor, but having related expertise. The community leaders are also expected to highlight major challenges linked to the community in front of the sponsor.

Community Members

Members are expected to perform actions that are linked to community objectives and highlight challenges to the leader. Members need to have a clear understanding that their growth is proportionally linked to organizational growth, therefore they need ensure that all actions are executed with the same passion and confidence. They also need to highlight new growth and learning opportunities. Some members may be interested in conducting a workshop, taking a training, and going onsite to work directly with clients, so these should be proposed to leaders who will assess and make decisions based on the interest of the community.

The community roles and responsibilities should be drafted and hosted in the Document Library. Further, this needs to be shared with all community members, leaders, sponsors, and heads, so that everybody takes ownership and meets the organizational objectives.

Perform Engagement Activities

Engagement topics are lists of engagement activities that a community is expected to perform in order to establish a potential community. Engagement activities include activities such as defining the community objective, creating a community plan, creating reusable knowledge resources, and proposing new ideas and new wins in each community. A community itself is an organization with a community leader as its head. The community should continue to work on their services and this should be linked to the community objective. A community objective could be creating SharePoint Online experts. To achieve this plan they might provide training and certification for community members, and proposed investment ideas could be developing a lab that will demonstrate use of SharePoint Online to customers.

Measure the Success of the CoP Initiative

We have to come to last part where we want to measure the community success and this is perhaps one of the difficult tasks as we have seen so far. Without a return on investment, any initiative is eventually a dead one. To measure success, one straightforward measure is to see returns achieved by investing in a community. For example, if a sponsor has invested 10 million USD in a community and returns are 12 million USD, we see that there is 2 million USD return. Not only this, but there are some intangible returns, such as reusable assets created by one community that benefitted other community and, as a result, the second community displayed a larger profit. Success would also depend on the new success stories created by the CoP initiative. If you want to measure success, define the parameters at the launch of the initiative and monitor them regularly.

Summary

Market research produced by Gartner said that employees get 50% to 75% of their relevant information directly from other people. Also, a McKinsey report found that lots of information and knowledge flows through informal employee networks compared to the official hierarchical and matrix structures. Both of these observations support the CoP initiative, which will help employees discover solutions, knowledge, and connections through their own ways in an organizational setup.

Organizations will have organizational and hierarchal barriers, business processes, and project specific barriers, local culture, time, and language barriers and, finally, isolated knowledge islands. SharePoint Communication sites is an ideal platform to overcome these barriers. SharePoint Communication sites will open knowledge horizons and enhance interpersonal communication beyond islands. Employees with different expertise will cross-fertilize in networks and foster innovations. The sites will access knowledge networks by providing access to tacit knowledge.

With SharePoint Communication sites, questions such as "How can I better connect with colleagues in a global company setting?" and "Who can I exchange experiences with on this promising technology trend?" can be answered.

In this chapter, we learned what the CoP initiates, how it will benefit organizations, and how we can implement it using SharePoint Communication sites. Features in Communication sites are simple to use in implementing such issues. Further, we saw a practical example of the CoP initiative and I believe you will find it useful. In the next chapter, we explore another landmark of Communication sites and we discover how it can be used to manage social knowledge.

CHAPTER 7

Social Knowledge Management Using Communication Sites

In the previous chapter, we had an opportunity to look at how Communication sites are useful in building and nurturing communities. These sites also create full-time collaborative experiences for each community member. With underlying Communication sites, the sustenance and development of different communities has become possible, all to achieve the company's goals. In this chapter, we focus on one of the specific aspects of community building—knowledge. A community must have access to knowledge in order to further its development. Knowledge management is a key principle that communities can use to harvest knowledge, reuse it, and create new knowledge for the growth of the community.

This chapter explains what knowledge management and social knowledge management are. Importantly, it also discusses how Communication sites help create and store knowledge assets that are important for business.

© Charles David Waghmare 2019
C. D. Waghmare, *Beginning SharePoint Communication Sites*,
https://doi.org/10.1007/978-1-4842-4203-2_7

Understanding Knowledge Management

Before going into the details, it's important to understand knowledge management from the layman's standpoint. See Figure 7-1.

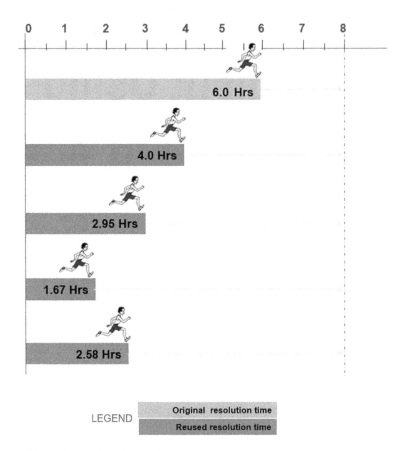

Figure 7-1. *Reusable knowledge assets*

In Figure 7-1, we see that once a solution was used, it was repeatedly used by others to fix new problems in order to become efficient and productive. Imagine you're working at the customer service operations of a credit card company, where you get thousands of queries from customers each day. Sometimes these queries are repeated, but the consultants are different and they don't know which other colleagues might have answered this question already. Further, due to the large number of consultants working at the customer service organization, some are trained to handled certain processes, while others take time due to the capacity management of the training program. In addition, due to rotational shifts, the same query is being asked in the morning, afternoon, and night to different consultants. It is a very complex issue. These queries are often trivial but the company is still spending plenty of money and is unable to innovate to deliver better results.

Knowledge management makes things easy and simple. Knowledge management is a process that allows you create, store, and reuse knowledge. Access to knowledge is also an important component, as knowledge should be open to all so that it can be accessed and used beneficially. This process can be implemented with the help of technologies such as SharePoint Online, Drupal, content management system (CMS), and others.

In Figure 7-1, we see how a solution, once it's implemented, is reused by others to be productive. In the example situation of the credit card customer service organization, a knowledge management system could store all the answers provided by the consultants and they could then be reused to answer future queries raised by new customers. This would improve efficiency and productivity and provide quick wins to customer problems. An efficient search would help consultants find knowledge as and when they need it. Not only this, but there should be encouragement to create new knowledge assets so that they can be reused.

Knowledge management will help you:

- Resolve issues easily using past experiences

- Learn continuously

- Increase your visibility

- Break physical and geographic barriers

- Make your opinion count

- Save time by not reinventing the wheel

- Network with the SMEs/be an SME

- Improve the quality of your deliverables

Helpful Arguments for Sharing Knowledge

When you work on a knowledge management (KM) program, there will be a lot of questions asked, such as how will knowledge management benefit an individual and entire organizations and what are the returns when a team participates in the KM program?

First, let's consider how an individual can benefit:

- Anyone providing valuable information to the team is demonstrating their confidence in the team and indicating openness and readiness to talk. The important thing is that somebody takes the first step.

- This is generally rewarded by the team, as others then share their knowledge. People who share information get a lot of very useful information in return.

- Instead of making people dispensable, it makes them interesting partners in discussion and cooperation.

How does the team benefit?

- A team grows together more if people trust each other. This makes the team stronger, both during high-stress periods and in displaying competent performance of team tasks.

- The increased capability of the team enhances its reputation. This in turn has a positive effect on the reputation and status of the individual team members.

- The working climate improves, and an atmosphere of trust emerges, which also quickly results in innovations.

What do the individual and the team have to do?

- Trust persists only if the individual's intellectual copyright is protected. Neither management nor other team members must be allowed to claim credit for other people's ideas. This destroys trust!

- Anybody who does good work and shows their trust must be rewarded. Esteem, praise, and promotion initiate positive feedback loops.

Constituents of Knowledge Management

As air is everywhere, so knowledge is everywhere. When two colleagues go for coffee and discuss project-related information that builds knowledge, when lots of knowledge is being exchanged during conference calls or audio conferences, when communications and emails to clients are shared, you are exchanging vital knowledge. When you interact with the system with some input, you get output, which is also knowledge. When people discuss topics over social networks, you find a lot of knowledge is exchanged. Social networks, blogs, wikis, and content and document systems are all places where you will find plenty of information being exchanged. They become the hub of knowledge. Normally, knowledge is shared and created when people interact with people, people interact with technology, and technology interacts with people. These form the constituents of knowledge management (see Figure 7-2).

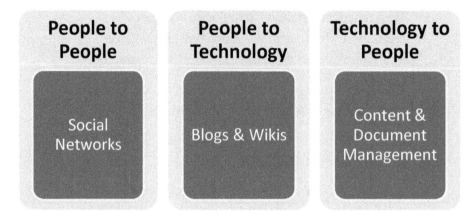

Figure 7-2. *Constituents of knowledge management*

The Knowledge Management Cycle

Knowledge management is a process that contains four steps to form a cycle. Knowledge being created, shared, accessed, and used forms a complete knowledge management cycle. What is the use of a knowledge asset if it is not used? Building reusable knowledge assets forms the complete cycle of knowledge management (see Figure 7-3).

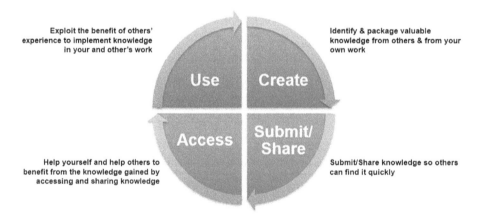

Figure 7-3. *Knowledge management lifecycle*

There are two different types of knowledge, as explained here:

- **Tacit knowledge**—This is understood consciously and applied to different situations. It is not evident, difficult to articulate, built from experience and action, and is shared through highly interactive conversations, storytelling, and shared experiences. For example, surveys and polls are rolled out to gather the tacit knowledge of employees.

- **Explicit knowledge**—This is articulated and formally presented, easily codified, documented, transferred, and shared. For example, operating manuals, process documents, procedures, product literature, and computer software.

Business benefits of knowledge management to deliver organization:

- Improves productivity of consultants and ensures error-free/first time right (FTR) workways

- Ensures new joiners adapt faster and thereby reduces impact on delivery to customer

- Improved SLAs and response time due to reduced information search time and drive standardization across processes

- Helps get access to Global Subject Matter Experts (SMEs) across an organization

- Ensures knowledge is provided at the point of need or at the moment of truth

- Focuses on driving culture of sharing and re-use of knowledge and an organizational body of knowledge for long-term business advantages

- Captures transactional knowledge, experiential knowledge, and external knowledge to meet all the needs of the consultants

- Helps bring several organizational entities closer by providing opportunities of social collaboration and standardized documentation structure

- Inspires an open, transparent work culture that respects new ideas and thereby encourages innovations in the organization

- Generates knowledge and intellectual capital for an organization

Era of Social Knowledge Management

Evolving technology has changed the way we manage processes. Web 2.0 technology, where users are exposed to features such as comment and share, has made them more social and collaborative. Traditional knowledge management was to create, share, access, and reuse, but with the social feature, this tradition has changed and now people have started discussing what knowledge they are creating. They often ask if anyone can help to find reusable assets and access knowledge assets. Social aspects and knowledge management has given birth to social knowledge management, which is a knowledge management system with web 2.0 features built-in. For example, a content management system such as Drupal can be integrated into Yammer to form a social knowledge management platform.

Knowledge management is professional and well recognized in the market. MAKE (Most Admired Knowledge Enterprise) is an international body that awards different types of organizations for successfully practicing knowledge management in their organizations. This award is given global-, geography-, and business-wise. There are individual country and regional MAKE awards. Organizations such as TCS, Infosys, Wipro, and Mindtree have been consistent winners of MAKE awards.

Knowledge Management with SharePoint Communication Sites

SharePoint Communication sites is a valuable product for doing knowledge management, as it helps create, store, and reuse knowledge in a simple manager. It also allows people to collaborate with knowledge assets. Not only that, but it also allows people to create taxonomy for knowledge so that it can accessed by users with minimum pain. In this section, we explore the different knowledge management techniques that can be effectively adopted using SharePoint Communication sites.

Build a Solution Database

Incident management is one of the challenging process to manage due to the service level agreements (SLAs) attached to it. Whenever an incident or fault occurs, the team has to fix the agreed timeframe as per the SLA or they will be penalized. There are teams that support this process 24X7 and during weekends to keep the system up and running. If you repeatedly violate incidents, you tend to lose your reputation with your customer. Consistent winners of MAKE awards have pioneered incident management by integrating it into knowledge management to make it successful. As a result, incidents are fixed on time, employee productivity goes up, and customer satisfaction is achieved.

A solution database (SDB) containing reusable solutions can be created in SharePoint Communication sites for people to access solutions of the previously resolved incidents. A solution database ensures that knowledge created through transactions (incidents) are captured, categorized, and stored in the solution database for future reuse. The solution database allows the user to search for existing solutions of past incidents, which can be reused for future incidents.

Reusable solutions can be created using a workflow in SharePoint Communication sites. Such a workflow will ensure that only the proper approval and precise solution will be available in the global pool for reuse. Incident management processes and knowledge management can be integrated to achieve powerful results. Successful organizations have modified their incident management process to such an extent that, whenever an incident is received, instead of working on it as everyone would expect, search in SDB is reusable and only if the search is unsuccessful, can the team go further and start working on it. Finally, in a situation in which there is no reusable solution, teams are advised to create a new solution so that it can be reused in the future. Here are some advantages of using SDB:

- Improves productivity through reduction in time for solving incidents

- Builds knowledgebases of reusable solutions for long-term advantages

- Authentic solutions ensure quality resolutions of any future incidents

- Quick and effective retrieval of required solutions at the time of need

- Increases service quality

- Frequently reused solutions lead to standard solutions and generic problems

- Drive sharing and reuse as cultural change

Some companies have associated a rating system to SDB, which means if you create a solution, you are bound to get points. And if the system is reused, you are bound to get more points. Such a technique of SDB has become easy and convenient using Communication sites.

Create Communication Sites a Hub for Best Practices

Why do people attend and participate in events, conferences, symposiums, and seminars? The answer is simple—to learn and understand best practices. We are aware of what we are doing but we are always interested in knowing what others are doing in order to innovate and learn.

The best practices or lead practices are business insights pertaining to any part of the value chain. In simple terms, they encapsulate knowledge on any improvement or articulate better ways of doing things for more effective results. For example, consider a MIS design, programming logic, process to effectively meet customer expectations, First-Time-Right (FTR) workways, training modules, and so on. By operational definition, any improvement that impacts business profitability by yielding revenue, reducing costs, and improving customer and employee satisfaction could be a best practice/lead practice. These practices will include only those that have been demonstrated in any part of the organization and are directly replicable. It will include but not be limited to case studies, Six Sigma projects, templates, and whitepapers.

Communication sites provide a Document Library webpart that can be used to store best practice documents and these can be shared across teams. This Document Library webpart can be used to store external knowledge, and this refers to any knowledge that comes from outside the organization. In simple terms, these are knowledge artifacts that are useful for employees for learning and application purposes but belong to other organizations.

Structured Document Management System

Organizations in the past were mismanaging their company documents, which were found in their employees' personal laptops, pen drives, mobile devices, and in their private email accounts. This is complete breach of information security. With SharePoint Communication sites, we can create a standard folder structure to host documents and manage permissions to them. This can be achieved primarily due to the Document Library webpart and others such as Yammer to collaborate and create forms to capture metadata information about documents. With such a solution, company-related documents are secure on the company infrastructure and can be accessed using a mobile app. That way, the information security risk is minimized. A good document management system will enable:

- Faster access to information

- Easily comprehensible document organization

- Common source for most recent and authentic information

- Improved decision making

- Less chance of errors

- Standard documentation practices, i.e., standard templates

- Reduce variability of documentation

- A quicker learning aid for new joiners

Ask Expert: Ask and You Shall Receive

With the people webpart and the employee profile feature available in SharePoint, you can create an expert program. As the name suggests, this functionality helps employees get answers to their queries from experts.

All the responses are stored in the database and are searchable for the subsequent answer seekers. Employees and experts will have options to provide tags to each query, which will be crucial for further searches. Experts will have to respond to queries in one week's time. The rating system makes this process efficient. For example, each query that's responded to will fetch 10 points for the expert and 2 points for the employees who posted the queries.

The process for the Expert finder and Ask Expert should be combined, as both processes have strong logical handshakes, per the business need. As a consistent working principle, SMEs will be identified by department heads or process owners. Whether the SMEs will have a role within a national boundary or a business unit boundary will be deliberated in detail with management. A strong argument in favor of assigning a role to the SMEs would be to ensure uniform deployment of processes, consistent standards of quality, and building a common delivery pool from the point of view of the knowledge processes.

Create an Experience of Social Collaboration by Using Features of Communication Sites

Social collaboration is all about promoting people-to-people collaboration in enterprises to harness collective intelligence. Many "community behavior" studies have revealed explicitly that it always helps to connect to an individual at a personal level. Knowing more about backgrounds, scholastics, interests, and so on, leads to more fruitful interactions. All this has led to the emergence of social collaboration. Social Collaboration tools at the enterprise level (also called as social computing) provide us with the ability to connect people to people, people to communities, and people to content. It becomes all the more relevant to have social collaboration tools in a scenario when a strong workforce with a diverse background operates from almost all the time zones. Here are the objectives of social collaboration:

- Connect people to people (P2P)

- Discover and tap into the power of communities

- Connect people, content, and ideas

- Facilitate free flow of information and ideas that trigger tendencies to innovate

The following key features or functionalities of social collaboration exist in SharePoint Communications sites as webparts:

- Personal profile

- Create manage communities

- Wiki or community page: collective authoring and document collaboration

- Power apps: to centralize your customized apps

- Share links, share calendars, and online surveys

Summary

In this chapter, we learned what knowledge management is and learned about the new era of KM, which is called social knowledge management. We also learned about the different knowledge management techniques that can be used to do KM and can easily be implemented using features of SharePoint Communication sites. Finally, if you are clear with most of the information in this chapter, you should be ready to do social KM using Communication sites.

CHAPTER 8

Create New Horizons of Digital Communication

So, far we have seen that the SharePoint Online's Communication sites are multipurpose. We have seen that Communication sites can be used for building digital Intranets, managing knowledge and information, developing internal websites for different departments, and creating collaborative experiences by integrating with Office 365 products such as Yammer, Outlook, teams, Stream, and OneDrive. We have come to the last chapter now and in this, we will go one step further and describe the news of communication using SharePoint Communication sites. Initially, we highlight traditional ways of communicating and see how SharePoint communication transforms traditional communication into digital with its ease of use. It allows you to create new horizons of digital communication.

Understanding Digital Communication

Originally, communication was mouth-to-mouth, as there were no channels to communicate information. Then came telephones and the printing press, by which communication was sent through papers and shared over telephones. With the evolution of the Internet, computers and mobile technology communication became advanced. Through these channels, anyone can communicate with anyone all over the world at any time. Social media channels led communication to another level and emerging technologies are continuing the world of digital communication.

Digital communication is communication in the form rich text, images, graphics, videos, and other elements of emergent technologies, which can be shared efficiently and to any audience. Communication that receives emails and contains different resources such as links, images, and videos is an example of digital communication. Another example is the communication we receive through internal collaboration platforms, such as Yammer. Today, people communicate their company's achievements on LinkedIn or Facebook, which are other examples of digital communication.

Using SharePoint Communication Sites for Digital Communication

After gaining an understanding of digital communication and having knowledge of SharePoint Communications sites from the previous chapters, the time has come to create SharePoint Communication sites for digital communication. As we have seen in the previous chapters, SharePoint communication is easy and simple to use and you will have no problem building digital communications in your organizations.

In any organization, internal communications are important to the functioning of the company. The team needs to be in the know in order to communicate the right information on time. In order to do this, the team also needs a set of tools to communicate in an effective manner and be able to collaborate with the end user community regarding published communication. The following sections include some tips whereby the internal communications team can use SharePoint Online to publish digital communication.

Use OneNote

Before sending communication, it is important to do brainstorming to hash out the objective of the communication, who the target audience is, what kind of views and opinions will be generated, whether there are enough visuals, what the frequency of the communication should be, and so on. You need to brainstorm with your team in order to plan effective communication. Using OneNote, you can brainstorm with your team to produce ideas and get the details of communications. Your team could be widespread across the world, but no worries about that, because OneNote is independent of time or geography and multiple users can share their ideas at once in OneNote. Since OneNote and SharePoint Communication sites are seamlessly integrated, you can create OneNote for each of your new communication channels. Once your ideas are established within your team, your ideas can be translated into communication by using different Communication site features. Your digital communication plan can be launched.

Use Yammer for User Collaboration

In Chapter 3, we discussed how Yammer can be effectively used with SharePoint Online to create collaborative experiences for end users. Using the Yammer webpart, you can easily add Yammer feeds to your Communication sites. Yammer and Communication sites work hand-in-hand to create digital communication with your end users. Any news, announcements, or updated publications on the Communication site can be shared with your Yammer group to get input or feedback from users. The internal communications team can remain engaged with users for different reasons, such as to ask for feedback, discover new topics for news, learn the benefits of news from end users, and determine what international communication to do to bring digitalization to their communication channels. The user community consists of experts, such as technologists, software engineers, testers, and business analysts. Internal communications can collaborate with such experts through Yammer and the team can write a series of articles about technology or engineering. In digital communication, end user reaction is important and this can be gathered and evaluated by using Yammer.

Use Webparts Effectively

In Chapter 4, we listed different webparts that the SharePoint Communication sites can offer in order to build digital communication. We will not discuss all of them, but we will look at some webparts that will help you build digital communication.

Hero Webpart

This webpart is used to showcase important news, information, or updates. Hundreds of different news sources are published daily on your Intranet sites, so you should strategize to collect the best and most useful news available to the user community. This webpart also allows you to add graphics to your top news to make it more visually appealing. The top news could be your financial report of the fiscal year, an interview with the CEO, an annual review from the leadership team, or top customer wins. If you communicate big news in the best manner, i.e. by showing it distinctively separate from other news, people will see and read it, as well as share their reactions.

Microsoft Stream

As we saw in Chapter 5, Microsoft Stream is a cloud-based Office 365 service used to share videos and animation in order to communicate messages or share knowledge. In this fast-paced world of digital communication, most users don't want to take the time to read and understand news. In fact, they will not bother to read anything that contains a huge amount of text. Today, the expectation from the user standpoint is that they want to understand news or published information in the smallest amount of time, with the minimum amount of reading effort, and they should be able to share this communication with others using features available at their fingertips.

Global organizations today have adopted digitized internal marketing strategies whereby they create 2-3 minute videos to communicate important messages. Leadership interviews, business highlights, services overviews, and technology trends are some of the topics that are communicated by using videos. Even a campaign launch message can be communicated using a video. Not only videos, but there are also animations used for communication.

In my experience, I had the opportunity to write an animation script to explain the success of the Yammer network. It had to be less than 90 seconds and be valid three years after it was launched, which meant the information could not become outdated in the future. This animation was launched and appreciated by users globally. The animation was shared using Yammer, which was central to placing and communicating its launch. There are videos and animations that are part and parcel of digital communication. Microsoft Stream can be used to host videos and the Stream webpart will help you display videos and animations to your user community.

People Webpart

Finding experts in your organization is also challenging and during crises, they are almost impossible to locate. Very few organizations in my opinion use the Expert Connect program. In one organization where I worked, there was a bigger focus on the Expert Connect program. There was a dedicated site where you could find a list of experts in various areas. Experts were selected through a careful evaluation process and expectations—such posting a blog and creating an expert story—were set for them on a regular basis. Experts who did not meet these expectations were frequently eliminated from the Expert Connect program. Due to the busy schedules of these experts, a team of bloggers worked with experts so that, on a weekly basis, they could create a blog entry. Experts were not only engaged internally but their engagement was also extended to the outside world depending on their availability. The idea of having an Expert Connect program was extended outside of the company as well to create social business and brand employees. If an external user's problem was fixed by these experts, this sometimes lead to business, called social business. The People webpart provides a wonderful opportunity to showcase experts in the organizations and get their maximum attention during times of crisis.

Microsoft Forms to Create to Surveys, Quizzes, and Polls

Determining what people think about published communication or information is an important aspect of digital communication. Most of the time, users will not able to express opinions by posting. In such situations, polls, surveys, and quizzes help gather tacit information about the user community and such knowledge can be used for improvement. Today, organizations spend millions to partner with companies and use their special survey tools to perform employee surveys. Normally, questions are shared with a survey company, which helps roll out the survey and produce the survey results.

We are not saying that spending millions on a third-party survey company is not worth it, necessarily, as this depends on your company needs and policies. However, if your Communication sites are providing you a webpart that could achieve similar objectives, why not try using and leverage it? Surveys, polls, and quizzes are often used during campaigns to engage users and all these three are available as webparts. Managing tacit knowledge and user engagement with surveys, forms, and polls is available at your fingertips.

Planner Webpart

Planner is an Office 365 service that's used to create plans and share them with a wider audience. When we execute a campaign or roll out communication, these activities often seem out of the blue and seem like they will die in a short span of time. The internal communications team normally has a plan, but does not have a channel to communicate that plan to a vast audience, or in some organizations, this plan is considered confidential. The goal is to create a digital communication experience so users know about these planned activities. Once the plan is finalized, the entire team can then be committed to roll out the plan and, if deadlines are not met, explanations will be provided to management. With Planner, you can create plans with your global team by considering their inputs. Once this is finalized, you can share the final version with your end user community.

Such a digital communication plan will make the end users realize that the communication business is a serious one and that the plan has come after groups of people worked on and remained committed to the plan. A communication plan typically covers campaigns, series, events, and monthly or weekly highlights. Such a plan will create a different image in front of the end user community. There can also be an internal plan during each campaign. This plan will launch the campaign announcement, publish marketing collaterals, run competitions, share polls, and publish campaign results. Planner is the standard way of working with plans and, unlike Excel where you have to maintain multiple versions, Planner organizes the data for you. SharePoint provides the Planner webpart so you can plan your digital communication in a digital way.

Twitter, Kindle, Bing Maps, Weather, and Embed

Up to this point, we have discussed how you can take work that you've created inside your workplace to a digital space. You can also engage people on non-work-related issues inside the workplace to make them more productive and control the content.

You can engage your employees using the Twitter, Kindle, Bing Maps, Weather, and Embed webparts. For example, say your employees are looking for weather updates so that they can plan their commute or business travels. Instead of going to an Internet site or doing a Google search, if you provide them with a Communication site, they can use SharePoint to do this instead.

As another example, people often break multiple times from work to get social media updates, such as to check their Twitter feeds. SharePoint provides a Twitter webpart so employees do not have switch devices to use Twitter, but can see their Twitter feeds in the Communication sites. Another advantage is that tweets published by the marketing and communication team can be linked to the organization and can be available to employees as well.

Google Maps is another application that is accessed by employees on a regular basis. SharePoint provides the Bing Maps webpart to find distance and directions. The Kindle webpart gives people an awesome experience to read the best books using the Kindle app.

Finally, all external content posted from your company from Facebook, Instagram, and LinkedIn can be managed from SharePoint. This could be information published from the Harvard Business Review, social media marketing reports, or Gartner or Forrester updates. You can bring all of this information into your single Communication site. This is really awesome stuff and creates a cohesive digital communication experience.

Office 365 Connector Webpart

To create an enhanced digital experience, the Communication sites offer a variety of apps to bring content from external and internal sources into the site page. The Office 365 Connector webpart uses connectors such as Asana, BitBucket, Facebook pages, GitHub and Enterprise, Google Analytics, Incoming Webhook, Jira, RSS, Salesforce, Stack Overflow, Trello, and User Voice.

Document Library, File Viewer, Quick Charts

SharePoint Communication sites offer you an easy way to share and view documents. In the early days, documents were hosted in file servers and their links were embedded into the communication. But with the Document Library and File Viewer, things have changed. You can insert a document you would like to share with your user community. In the Document Library, users can create, edit, and share documents to SharePoint sites and they do not have to download them. With File Viewer, you can show a preview of documents or image files. Do not have to rely on Excel or PowerPoint presentations to create graphs. With Quick Charts, you can directly create graphs in your SharePoint Communication sites. The SharePoint sites have all the tools you need to create a rich digital experience.

Image Gallery

This webpart allows you to share pictures with your audience. Simply drag and drop pictures into this webpart. Once you have stacked images, you can reorder them with beautiful layouts, such as the Tiles layout and the Carousel layout. In the Carousel layout, you can set whether to automatically cycle through images you have selected for the carousel. You can also select the speed.

Highlighted Content Webpart

If you are interested in what is inside your Document Library, sites, or subsites, the Highlighted Content webpart is the solution to display an overview of what is inside. Using this webpart, you can dynamically display content from your Document Library, sites, or site collections, or even content from throughout the site. By default, this webpart will show the most recent document and if there is none, then you have to create or upload them. You can also choose layouts such as Cards, List, Carousel, or Filmstrip.

Link Webpart

With this webpart, you can add links to websites or documents that are hosted on OneDrive, SharePoint, or Box. When you add an URL, you will see a thumbnail preview of the link.

Upload Images Using the Image Webpart

You can include images in your Communication sites using the Image webpart. Using this webpart, you can also include text related to an image or even place text over an image, configure the aspect ratio, and crop image and rotate images as needed. You don't really need a picture editor to do all this, as the Image webpart provides nearly all features that a picture editor has.

Rich Text Webpart

This webpart has contains awesome options to make your communication look modernly digital. It has table and formatting features that are similar to Microsoft Word. Its formatting features consist of Undo and Redo, clear formatting from the selected text, choose from 10 font sizes, change the font color using standard or theme colors (theme colors change to reflect the theme of the site), add a highlight color, use strikethrough, use subscript and superscript, indent text, insert a table and choose table styles and alignment, hyperlink links and tables, choose table styles, and insert and delete rows. You can also set the alignment, such as left, right, centered, and justified.

List Webpart

This webpart allows you to create a list of your items, which can be customized as per your requirements. You can add a title, create a view, and even use a different size. You can view, filter, sort, and group the list, or go to the full list by clicking See All. Additionally, formatted columns and nested groups created in the source list are shown in the webpart.

News Webpart

In your organization, you can create visually appealing news for your teams, business units, and for the entire organization. You can create news for your partners as well. With the News webpart, you can create eye-catching news regarding status updates, announcements, new customer wins, leaders remarks, promotions, and acquisitions of new organizations. You can include graphics and rich text formatting. Once you publish the news, it becomes available on the SharePoint Communication site and on other SharePoint sites wherever you indicate. The default layout of published news is side-by-side, which is a two-column list of stories (see Figure 8-1).

Figure 8-1. *Side-by-Side layout*

You can change this layout to a List layout, which shows news posts in a single column (see Figure 8-2).

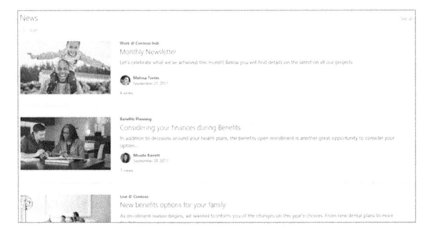

Figure 8-2. *List layout*

Figure 8-3 shows a layout with columns of stories in thumbnails, plus a sidebar of headlines of additional stories.

Figure 8-3. *Columns of stories with thumbnails and an information layout*

Figure 8-4 shows the top story layout. It includes a large image space and three additional stories.

Figure 8-4. *Top story layout*

Working with the News webpart, you will find options to add internal or external sources of news. They can be added as URLs and shared via email with a designated group of people, which can include external contacts as well.

Quick Link Webpart

With this webpart, you can quickly "pin" items to your page for easy access. You can add text to describe a link and display links in Compact or Filmstrip forms, as shown in Figures 8-5 and 8-6.

Figure 8-5. *Compact link*

Figure 8-6. *Filmstrip link*

With the Quick Links webpart, you can add links from OneDrive, SharePoint, Yammer, and other Office 365 services. With Quick Links, you can create FAQ documents, task lists, and pages containing useful or helpful links.

Create Organizational, Team, or Business Unit Events

Normally, to book events, we might use Outlook, but now you will not do that, as with the Events webpart, you can schedule events in your organization. When creating an event, you supply information such as when the event is scheduled, where it will take place, a description about the event, the type of event, such as meeting, work hours, business, holiday, and so on. If you have people you'd like to highlight for this event (such as contacts, special guests, or speakers), you can add their names to the event description. Only users within your organization can be added.

Forms in Communication Sites

If you want to organize team outings and understand where people want to go and which day they prefer, you can use the Polls feature to do this. However, it's better to use forms, which allow you to create responses more quickly and show the desired results in a consolidated format (see Figure 8-7).

Figure 8-7. *Response from a form*

Summary

The objective of this chapter was to build new horizons of communication using SharePoint communication. This is done using webparts. You learned about many webparts in this chapter that can help you communicate effectively. This can all be done with minimal effort and using out-of-box functionalities. There is very little extra coding needed.

With this, we have come to the end of this experience with SharePoint Communication sites, which was launched by Microsoft in 2018. Through this book, you are ready to use your Communication sites effectively. I hope you have enjoyed reading this book. Feel free to share comments and feedback using `charles.waghmare@gmail.com`. Best wishes on collaborating and communicating effectively using Communication sites.

Index

A

Agile scrum master, 37
Automatic software updates, 94
Azure active directory team, 111

B

Benefits, digital Intranets
    audience, 70
    augments collaboration, 70
    business operations and
        management, 69
    communication in time, 68
    cost-saving solution, 69
    employee communication, 67
    employee engagement, 70
    employee productivity, 68
    web publishing, 69
Bing maps, webpart, 146
Bring Your Own Device (BYOD), 90
Business unit events, 153

C

Carousel layout, 147
Cloud-based service, 1
Cloud first, 95

Cloud technology
    BYOD, 90
    competitive edge, 94
    data loss, 93
    data privacy, 92
    data quality, 91
    disaster recovery, 92
    employee collaboration, 91
    flexibility, 89
    insights, 90–91
    security, 88
    software updates, 94
    startups, 89
    sustainability, 94
    zero operating cost, 88
Collaborate, connect, and share, 73
Communication and
    accessibility, 72
Communication and collaboration
    campaign, 39
    facilities management, 35–36
    human resources, 27–28
    IC, 29–32
    leadership communication, 40
    smaller and larger
        groups, 37–38
    subdepartment, building, 28–29

© Charles David Waghmare 2019
C. D. Waghmare, *Beginning SharePoint Communication Sites,*
https://doi.org/10.1007/978-1-4842-4203-2